FORGING AHEAD

A HISTORY OF TOOLEY'S BOATYARD

By Matthew Armitage

To Iris
A great visit.

Matt

21-6-23

A catalogue record for this book is available
from the British Library.

ISBN – 978-0-9570151-8-0

Printed in the United Kingdom

Windlass Publishing Limited (Oxford)
12 Broad Field Road, Yarnton, Oxford,
OX5 1UL, United Kingdom.

CONTENTS

FOREWORD

Tooley's Boatyard in Banbury has for me a personal importance. My own narrowboat was built here in 1990, by Barrie Morse, who at that time held the lease for the Boatyard.

Seen from the canal towpath – or indeed from the canal itself – the yard looks nothing much. A black and white sign proclaims its existence, but its contours seem to be blended with the enormous Castle Quay shopping complex which effectively separates the canal (it reached Banbury in 1778) from the attractive old market town itself.

Matthew Armitage in his book goes into the changing story of the Boatyard; from its wooden boat-building days, through to its development by the Tooley family to cope with diesel-engine craft – necessitating a forge, a carpenter's shop, a belt-driven mechanical workshop, extensive chandlery and the oldest drydock on the inland waterways. I said, 'the changing story', but in fact in many ways the yard continues to uphold the principles of traditional skills as laid down by George and Herbert Tooley at the very beginning of the 20th century.

Tom Rolt, the engineer/historian/writer to whom those involved in the preservation of our canal system owe so much, designed, fitted out and decorated his famous narrowboat *Cressy* in the Boatyard, under the guiding hand of Herbert Tooley. When the job was finished George Tooley snr, in dark suit and bowler hat, stood beside Tom on his maiden voyage up the Oxford Canal.

Custodians of our canal history, like that of our railways, tend rather to be people of my own senescent generation. To find a relatively young man like Matthew so deeply involved with the fascinating story of Tooley's, and so concerned with its practical use today, is both encouraging and exciting.

Timothy West

ACKNOWLEDGEMENTS

Starting out as 'The Banbury Dockyard' over two hundred years ago, who could possibly have thought it would have survived throughout this time as a continuously working boatyard and forge? This book is a tribute to all of the owners, workers and people who, over the centuries, have dedicated themselves to its unique place in Banbury's history. Although my place in 'Tooley's' continuous journey is relatively recent, the last sixteen years of the yard's history have been fascinating and challenging in equal measure. There are many people who have helped me along the way, so many in fact that if I were to mention them all, we'd need a whole new chapter! Nevertheless, there are some I feel need a special mention.

My personal journey on the waterways started out on the restaurant boat *Rosamund the Fair*, and later at the Castlemill Boatyard, Jericho, Oxford. For all the good times and fond memories from that time, I'd like to thank Tim and Sophia Matthews. The lessons I learned during those early days provided me with the skills and confidence needed to operate and manage such a special site as Tooley's.

It is fair to say that Pete and Di Downer have played a pivotal role in the preservation and safeguarding of crucial parts of the yard's history. Their personal knowledge, and preservation of historic items relating to the Tooleys period has been invaluable. I can't thank them enough for their help with this book.

More recently, Sarah Jackson and Jamie Simmons have been remarkable friends to the Yard. They realised that I needed help with the business at a time when I needed it most. Mostly unpaid, their support, drive, hard work and ideas have been crucial during these recent challenging times. Dan and Sarah Clacher, for all their help and support during some demanding periods recently, and their assistance with this book. Thanks also to Jenny Lawrence for using her considerable design skills to assemble this book and to her father, Len, for editing the text.

Finally, and perhaps most importantly, for my wife, Anne, for supporting me and putting up with my absences during the very long hours that have been spent at Tooley's over the years.

INTRODUCTION

It's difficult for many people to consider that a few muddy canals cut through the countryside of England over two hundred years ago, has anything to do with the development of their smartphone or the moon landings in the 1960s. Yet the 'one small step' of building these rudimentary waterways was indeed a 'giant leap for mankind'.

Canals were the sprouting acorn seed, which became the mighty oak of the industrial revolution. Without them it's impossible to imagine the development and breathtakingly rapid industrial and scientific world we see today. In this book, Matthew Armitage, the director of the centuries old Tooley's Boatyard, provides us with a fascinating story which puts this humble, albeit listed, ancient monument at the centre of our current technological age.

Matthew has been the director of the oldest continuously working boatyard on the Inland waterways, in the United Kingdom, since 2002. His personal journey to Tooley's Boatyard is fascinating. He has a background in archaeology, having been involved in digs and excavations of many lost sites similar to Tooley's over a period of eight years. His passion for the waterways is also deeply rooted. He can boast seven generations of Thames watermen and lightermen in his family history and he was taught boat handling skills by Bill Boswell, a veteran member of one of the last boating families on the waterways.

Matthew began his boating career in 1990, literally learning the ropes on the restaurant boat, *Rosamund the Fair*, on the River Thames and the Oxford Canal. He worked his way up and became a Department of Transport Boat Master, as well as a director in the company. During this time, he trained eight people to achieve their Boat Master licences.

By coincidence, *Rosamund the Fair* had been regularly serviced at Tooley's during the 1990s. Before taking on Tooley's, Matthew had negotiated with British Waterways to set up and manage the controversial boatyard at Jericho in Oxford, which is now earmarked for significant development following years of division and debate about its future.

He acknowledges that his achievements on the waterways have been managed with the help and assistance of friends along the way. In particular, the founder of the restaurant boat, *Rosamund the Fair*, Timothy Matthews and his wife Sophia Goodford, deserve special mention. It was working on the restaurant boat that Matt's waterways career really began. With Tim and Sophia, he negotiated taking on the Jericho Boatyard and later Tooley's.

Figure 1: NB Rosamund the Fair at Banbury Canal Day

In addition, Matthew is a skilled boat engineer, a qualified mechanic and a coded welder. After seeing someone losing a thumb at Osney Lock on the River Thames, he set up a Royal Yachting Association (RYA) Training Centre and has been a principal of this school for over twenty years, teaching boat handling courses.

Whilst he is an authority on the history of the boatyard, he also has an eye on the future. He is determined to see the working yard thrive and continue to succeed, despite the many potential problems ahead. He recognises that it may have seen off the Napoleonic era, the rise of the railways and road freight and even two world wars, but today's trials and struggles present their own, unique challenges.

Anyone with an interest in the canals and rivers of the United Kingdom is likely to be familiar with the work and life of the writer and engineer, Tom Rolt. The founder member of the Inland Waterways Association and arguably the saviour of the growing modern-day waterways network, Rolt has a very close association with Tooley's. His lifelong relationship with the yard is well chronicled and has doubtless cemented the continuing fascination for the skills and talents of boat engineers, past and present.

In 1968, L T C Rolt observed in the opening of his book Green and Silver,

'… for a thorough knowledge of the past can add immeasurably to our appreciation of the present.'

Matthew is acutely aware of Tom Rolt's place in the contemporary history of the waterways and covers his links with Tooley's later in this book. He is also mindful of the affection many have for this jewel in Banbury's crown and has taken this opportunity to bring the past right up to date with this absorbing new story of Tooley's Boatyard.

BACKGROUND

Tooley's Boatyard was once a thriving centre for horse drawn wooden boats. Unlike so many other yards which are now long gone, Tooley's has been in continuous operation since it was built in 1778. It has a proud heritage and history which has charmed and captivated visitors for many years.

Situated in the centre of Banbury in northern Oxfordshire, the yard could easily be missed as it nestles under the huge, modern Castle Quay shopping centre. The contrast between the old and the new is stark. Tooley's is listed as an ancient scheduled monument; it even has a blue plaque outside commemorating Tom Rolt, which hopefully secures its future, whatever changes lay ahead for the town.

In the 18th and 19th centuries small boat building and repair yards were common, and there were at least three in Banbury. Shown below, is an advert from 1788 which was placed in Jackson's Oxford Journal asking for someone to build boats. The first recorded occupier of the Banbury dockyard is referred to, in the Birmingham University Archaeological Recording of 2000, as a 'Mr Evans' although it's not known if the yard was named after him at that time.

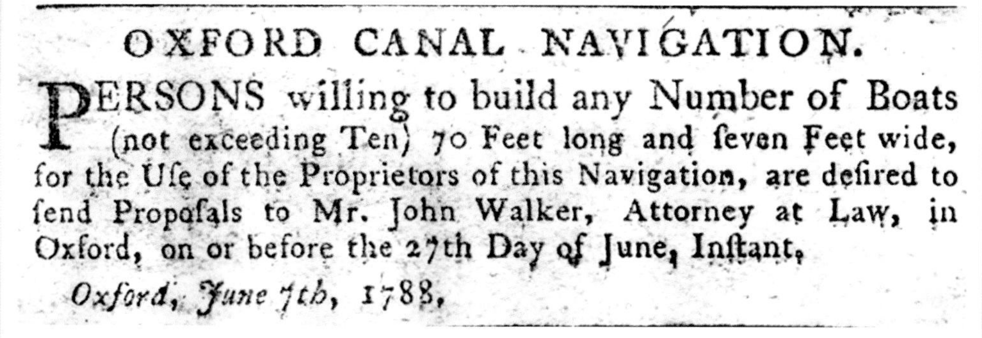

OXFORD CANAL NAVIGATION.

PERSONS willing to build any Number of Boats (not exceeding Ten) 70 Feet long and seven Feet wide, for the Use of the Proprietors of this Navigation, are desired to send Proposals to Mr. John Walker, Attorney at Law, in Oxford, on or before the 27th Day of June, Instant,

Oxford, June 7th, 1788,

Figure 2: Jackson's Oxford Journal advert from 1788

It was established to build and repair the wooden horse-drawn narrowboats which plied the newly constructed canal network, vital to the development of the burgeoning Industrial Revolution.

Later records show the boatyard in the hands of Thomas Cotton, who apparently built eleven boats, as reported in an extract from Cake and Cockhorse in 1805. According to the Birmingham University archaeological report of 2000, it changed hands many times over the coming years, with Benjamin Roberts shown from 1837 to 1864, followed by W J A Chard, then the Neal family until 1900. It wasn't until around 1900 that the yard established its eponymous title, when the Tooley family took over and ran it continuously until 1987. Whilst there are no definitive records or deeds showing the exact date of the Tooleys tenure, a number of anecdotal references survive. In particular is Herbert Tooley's own interview with Waterways World magazine when he refers to George senior taking over the dock around 1900. He goes on to say that they purchased the narrowboat *Providence* as a 'change' boat around this time. This strongly implies that they needed this boat to supply to customers as a temporary working craft whilst work was being carried out on their narrowboat in the dock. Moreover, narrowboat *Providence* is registered to George Tooley at Banbury in 1901.

Three generations of Tooleys; Emmanuel, George senior, George junior and Herbert, all played their part in its growth and development. Their exploits and ventures are covered in more detail later. Originally, the yard ran as two separate businesses, as a dry dock and a forge. However, they worked together to provide a service of building and repairing narrowboats.

The Tooleys continued the tradition of working on horse-drawn wooden boats, having built twelve wooden narrowboats between 1900 and 1928. Herbert Tooley refers to this period of activity in a Waterways World interview in 1982. However, big changes were emerging in boat building methods in the early part of the twentieth century. As engines were introduced as a power source, the Tooleys quickly adapted to the new environment. Using their long established skills, they were adept at introducing fresh and innovative approaches to emerging issues. They were far from profligate though, and would always seek ways to re-use materials and solve problems in the most cost efficient way. Today, they would be regarded as leading conservationists and proponents of the most ecological way of working. As we cover the workings of the yard in more detail, their distinctive approach becomes clear.

In 1998, the yard was closed whilst work began on the multi-million pound Castle Quay shopping development. Nevertheless, its historical and cultural importance was recognised in the full scale archaeological assessment conducted by Birmingham University, referred to above. The site was drawn, photographed and meticulously recorded. Artefacts were removed for examination and safe keeping during the contemporary building work and replaced in their original positions, once the site was regenerated. Published in August 2000, it is worth noting the report's conclusions,

'In several important ways the development of the boatyard was also a reflection of the unique culture of the boat people, and specifically of the character of the Tooley family. Here, concepts such as craftsmanship, versatility, and a devotion to the recycling of any materials were crucial, notions that Tom Rolt highlighted in his book 'Narrow Boat' (1944)...'

Figure 3: Development building around the yard. NB Rill in the background

CHAPTER ONE

THE OXFORD CANAL

Figure 4: The Oxford Canal at Kidlington

C anals have been around for a very long time. Initially used as a crude form of irrigation, they eventually developed into a far more sophisticated means for transporting goods and passengers. Incredibly, one of the earliest man made canal systems dates back to the fifth century BC in Beijing, China. Simple pound locks, a stretch of water between two rudimentary locks, also originated from China and date even further back to the tenth century BC. In the United Kingdom, the earliest recorded canals date back to the Roman era.

Despite their ancient roots and heritage, it wasn't until the 1700s that the canal system as we know it today, emerged as an unlikely precursor to our modern way of living. As the early commercial needs of the industrial revolution developed, the drive for coal and raw materials became acute. The solution at that time was the innovative use of new and successful techniques in canal building.

At that time, the transport system in Britain was slow and expensive. Goods were either taken the long way around the coast or they were pulled in small quantities by horse drawn wagons or pack horses, along old unmaintained roads left over from Roman times.

In 1759, the Duke of Bridgewater was authorised by Parliament to build a canal from his coal mine in Worsley to Manchester. Having visited France as part of the 'Grand Tour' in his youth, the Duke was inspired by the Canal du Midi. Built in the mid to late seventeenth century by the engineer Pierre Paul Riquet under the reign of Louis XIV, it was a staggering feat. It ran for 240 kilometres (150 miles) forming a link across southern France between the Mediterranean and Atlantic seas. It is one of the oldest canals in Europe still in operation and is a UNESCO World Heritage Site. Having seen what was possible in France, the Duke was convinced something similar, if not better, could be built in Britain. Nevertheless, the driving force behind his ambition was to transport his coal quickly and efficiently, thus making his mines more profitable.

With the help of one of his estate managers, John Gilbert, the Duke employed the services of the engineer James Brindley and the Bridgewater Canal was constructed and completed in 1776. This impressive canal had an aqueduct and tunnels going directly in to the coal mines, which made loading the boats easier. In Manchester, the new canal made distributing the coal simpler and locally the price of coal fell.

Due to the success of the Bridgewater Canal and much support for his work, Brindley compiled plans to build a network of canals linking the four navigable rivers; the Severn, Mersey, Humber and Thames. This was named the Grand Cross (shown below).

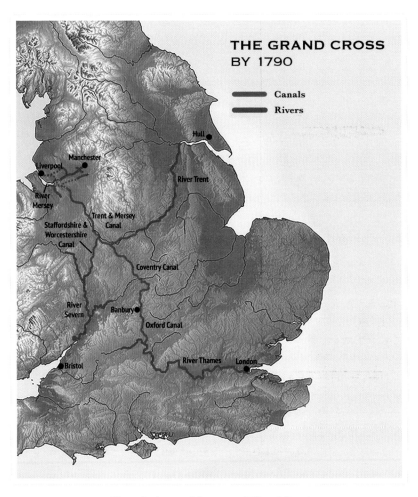

Figure 5: A map of the proposed 'Grand Cross'

In order to connect to the River Thames, the building of the Oxford Canal was authorised in 1769. Once again, the inspiration was the transportation of much needed coal. Warwickshire coalfields were highly productive and could easily service the needs of growing towns and cities to the south such as

Banbury and Oxford. The Oxford Canal Company was commissioned and work began. This was a mammoth project and despite experience in northern canal building, the time and money needed to complete the Oxford was vastly underestimated.

Figure 6: Canal construction unknown date

The initial survey and construction was supervised by James Brindley, who was assisted by his brother in law, Samuel Simcock. When Brindley died in 1772, Simcock took over and completed the project. Beginning in the north to connect the Coventry Canal, the Oxford Canal had only gone as far south as Napton-on-the-Hill, still within Warwickshire, by 1774 at which time the company was already running out of money.

It was to take a further four years before it reached Banbury in 1778. The opening on March 30th is recorded in the local newspaper as a day spent in festivities. The first freight of about 200 cauldrons of coal was ushered to the new wharf, "amidst the loudest acclamations of a prodigious number of spectators". It was this same year that Tooley's, or as it was then, the Banbury Dockyard, later Boatyard, began its long history.

Figure 7: Oxford Canal Banbury aerial view 1920s

Figure 8: Jackson's Oxford Journal 1788 advert for employment

Eventually, more money was raised and the canal pushed on to Oxford, opening on January 1st 1790, the first boat having the band of the Oxfordshire Militia on board. This section of the canal was built as cheaply as possible. Lift or swing bridges were often used instead of brick ones and narrow, deep locks were built with single gates. Seen as a quick and cheap solution, a stretch of the River Cherwell was used rather than cut new channels. Ultimately, it proved to be a false economy as the whole route would occasionally find itself ransomed by the vagaries of a lively river. Flooding, fast current flow and weather patterns along this stretch, could hold up valuable cargoes for days or even weeks.

The first connection to the River Thames was provided by 'Duke's Cut' near Wolvercote, Oxford in 1789. It was commissioned by George, the fourth Duke of Marlborough, who was a major shareholder in the Oxford Canal Company. The income from the canal helped the Duke with the upkeep of his ancestral home, nearby Blenheim Palace.

Figure 9: Dukes Cut lock looking back to the Oxford Canal from the Thames

This completed an important trade route connecting the Midlands to London. Now coal could be moved quickly in large quantities and for the next fifteen years, the Oxford Canal became one of the most profitable trade links in Britain. The Duke of Bridgewater's mines went into profit and as the canals boomed, so did the other companies who needed their fuel and goods transported. At its peak, there were well over 4000 miles of navigable waterways and over 30 million tons of goods were being transported by narrowboat every year. Canal mania had been born.

In 1805, the Grand Junction Canal was completed. This provided a much more direct link between the Midlands and London and led to a decline in traffic on the Oxford Canal. The Oxford Canal Company protected itself by charging very high tolls for their five and a half miles stretch between Braunston and Napton. This became the link between the Warwick and Napton Canal and the Grand Junction Canal, making it part of the busy direct route between Birmingham and London.

In the 1820s, the Oxford Canal company modernised the northern part between Braunston and Coventry. The canal was straightened, cutting almost fourteen miles from the original winding route. Though expensive, the project proved worthwhile and profitable. Whilst the Oxford Canal maintained a reasonable profit right through to the twentieth century, this was mostly due to the more lucrative northern section. As the Grand Union Canal took more trade to London via its quicker and wider route, trade on the southern section of the Oxford Canal declined.

Oxford City centre once boasted a very busy and thriving canal basin. It was here that the canal came to its final destination before joining the River Thames. Most of the cargo coming to the city would be unloaded here. At its height it would be alive with narrowboats loading and unloading their valuable cargoes, before heading on to London or back up to Birmingham. By the 1930s, trade was in decline and in 1937 William Morris, famous for Morris Motors and later known as Lord Nuffield, bought the canal basin. By 1951, the basin was no longer in use and was filled in to facilitate the building of Nuffield College. The main part of the basin is now a car park leased to Oxford City Council. Canal enthusiasts continue to petition for a return of the area to its original state.

Today, the Oxford Canal is regarded as one of the most beautiful stretches of waterway in the country. It is well used, and well loved by boaters, walkers, cyclists and fishermen throughout the year. A short walk along any of its towpaths is full of colour, vibrancy and an abundance of flora and fauna.

Despite the period of decline in the mid 1900s, Tooley's Boatyard endured and as we shall see, sometimes only just. Dark clouds regularly gathered over the yard, with the constant threat of closure and even demolition ever near.

Figure 10: A painting by 'Valerie Petts' of the view from Marsh Footbridge looking south

CHAPTER TWO

NARROWBOATS

Figure 11: NB Blackcountryman freshly painted in the dock

he engineer, James Brindley, needed boats that could fit his new canal system. He designed boats that were narrow enough to fit through the locks, long enough to take cargo and of a weight that could be pulled by a single horse. The narrowboat, unique to England, was born of necessity. Early narrowboats were normally made from elm bases and oak sides, and incredibly, these wooden boats were still being built until the 1960s. By the 1800s, steel and iron boats were more common. Although engines became the norm in narrowboats, horses were still used until the middle of the 1900s.

The Oxford Canal, being a narrow beam, only accommodates narrowboats with a maximum length of 72ft, and a width of 7ft (22m x 2.1m). Typically, modern steel narrowboats tend to be around 6ft 10ins (2.08m) wide as this is now the width of the narrowest lock in the canal system.

In the past, the narrow-beamed boats were called long boats or barges. It's important to clear up a much debated issue regarding the names given to these boats and the conventions that apply today. Most modern, steel hulled vessels are referred to as 'narrowboats' (one word). Traditional, load carrying, often wooden craft, sometimes called heritage boats are generally referred to as narrow boats (two words). For the ease of reading and to avoid confusion, all of these types of vessel are referred to as 'narrowboats' throughout this book. The traditional narrowboats were originally bow hauled by groups of men, often the navigators left over from the building of the canals, many of whom hung around the public houses waiting for their next job. Despite their physical strength and capabilities, men were soon replaced by horses.

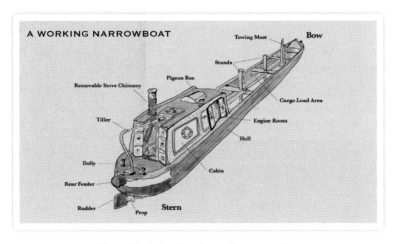

Figure 12: A drawing of a working narrowboat

Horses were capable of moving around fifty times as much weight in a boat as they could pull in a cart on the old roads. Three people were needed on board the narrowboat; one to steer, one to drive the horse down the tow path and a third to work the locks. Working a horse drawn boat was extremely hard. It was physically demanding, with long working days. The horse needed to be fed and watered regularly. They would tire after a long day on the towpath and needed to rest and be stabled overnight.

Other disadvantages of horse-drawn narrowboats occurred when negotiating tunnels. The horses would have to be un-hitched and led around the tunnel whilst the boaters 'legged it' through. Legging required the boaters to lie on a plank placed across the width of the boat, which allowed their legs to physically work the boat through, exhausting!

Figure 13: A young girl leading her narrowboat's horse

Towpath damage by heavy horses was also a constant headache for the canal companies. The vital pathways running alongside the canals had to be kept in a good state of repair, if long and costly delays were to be avoided. Continuous maintenance was expensive and ate into the businesses profits. Bank erosion and towpath wear has been a constant headache throughout the history of the canals. When powered vessels eventually replaced horses, their increased speed put a considerable strain on the watersides. Boats produced a greater wash which rapidly eroded the rudimentary bankside construction.

Whilst these methods of moving freight might seem antiquated and old fashioned to modern observers, their impact on the economy and wider society cannot be overstated. In his book, The Canal System of England, Hugh Gordon Thompson, writing at the turn of the 20th Century, sums up the dramatic changes perfectly,

'Before the completion of these great schemes the natural increase of commerce in the middle of the 18th century was greatly hindered by the heavy expense and the lack of adequate means of conveying produce to the ports. Thus, about the year 1750, the cost of goods by road between Manchester and Liverpool was 40 shillings per ton, but by the Mersey and Irwell the water rate was only 12 shillings per ton, and after the opening of the Bridgewater Canal the cost was reduced to 6 shillings per ton, and a better service was given than that provided by either of the aforementioned routes. Again, the cost of transport of coal which up to this time was carried by packhorse from Worsley to Manchester, and which had been from 6 to 8 shillings per ton, was reduced to 2 shillings and sixpence per ton on the canal.'

Perhaps the best contemporary analogy for this fundamental change from packhorse to narrowboat, is the modern difference between dial-up and fibre optic broadband speeds. It's an interesting thought that canal and narrowboat developments were the spark that burst the industrial revolution into life and set us on the path to today's technological age.

Pay and Conditions

A boat captain's pay was based on the tonnage carried on each trip. Loading and unloading of cargoes were down to the captain and his crew. From this, they had to pay the wages of their crew. This cost, and that of having to maintain a home on land coupled with the competition from road haulage, may well have led to the trend for family units to move out of their houses. By the 1830s they started to move on to the boats and the whole family learned to support life afloat. Further financial pressure mounted when boatmen's wages dropped as rail competition took hold.

Families lived in incredibly cramped quarters in the back of the boat, which was known as the 'Boatman's Cabin'. This was an area of only 9ft x 7ft (2.75m x 2.13m) The bulk of the boat's structure was needed for cargo to maximise the economic return, whilst making room for the crew was regarded as a luxury. Boaters became ingenious at living together in such a confined space, utilising every inch to the maximum, with fold-out and hide away tables and beds. There was always a small bottle stove or cooking range which would have been kept permanently lit and sporting a kettle for making tea, the staple drink.

Figure 14: The rear painted section of NB Venice in the dock

To some, this might be considered romantic, but the work was physically demanding and far from easy. The annual Report of the Local Government Board 1885, reveals the reality of life afloat,

'Bargemen, watermen and lightermen, between the ages 25 and 65 were almost twice as likely to be killed than agricultural labourers.'

Attempts to improve the lot of the children of boating families were established by a variety of Canal Boat Acts. Significant change came with the act of 1877, which restricted life on board. The 1884 Act required local authorities to ensure that boat children attended school, but enforcement was sporadic and difficult. Boat children were not always received favourably by teachers and local children. Later, the 1920 Boat Children's Education Act, required boat children to attend school 200 days a year. There were supposedly limits on the number of children permitted to live aboard but these were often flouted. More children meant more hands to help.

One of the best known and last working families on the canals were the Skinners. Joe and Rose Skinner worked their narrowboat, a 70ft (21m) Number 1, called *Friendship* throughout the southern network. They bought it in 1924 for £300 and in 1928 they bought a second boat, *Elizabeth*, which they worked as a pair. These boats were towed by mules named Dolly and

Figure 15: The back cabin of NB Friendship painted at Tooley's in the 1950s

Dick, as Joe much preferred mules to horses for canal work. They sold *Elizabeth* in 1937 but continued moving coal from the East Midlands to Banbury for decades to come. It was whilst here in the 1950s, that the back cabin of *Friendship* was painted at Tooley's, the distinctive style clear to see in this photograph.

The following newspaper report (p25) from December 1957 tells the tragic story of how the Skinners began to lose their appetite for life on the water. The heart-rending story of how Dolly had slipped into the canal and caught pneumonia must have been hard for the Skinners. Using a nautical term, the reporter records that they were 'becalmed' (unable to move) at Sutton Stop near Coventry as Dolly had died. They could, of course, have had a motor fitted to *Friendship* but as the report observes, 'Mr Skinner, who has worked on the canals since boyhood, could have had a boat with an engine long ago, but he preferred Dolly.' They retired soon after and moved to a house close to the waterways. Joe died in 1975 aged 82, his wife Rose following him a year later aged 77.

Luckily, *Friendship* was rescued by The Coventry Canal Society in 1977 and can now be seen in all her glory at the National Waterways Museum in Ellesmere Port.

Figure 16: Joe and Rose Skinner on NB Friendship

Figure 17: A painting of a photograph of Dolly the mule taken by Sonia Rolt
at Tooley's Boatyard painted by Jacqueline Arriaga da Cunha

Figure 18: Joe Skinner with Dolly the mule

'Dolly,' Last Narrow Boat Mule, is Dead

COUPLE ARE 'BECALMED'

"DOLLY" the mule—last of the narrow boat working horses in the Midlands—is dead. And without her, 65 years old Joe Skinner and his wife Rose are "becalmed" at Sutton Stop, Longford, Coventry, in their boat "Friendship."

They will have to buy another animal—mule or horse—or hire one, if possible. In the mean-time, they may have to surrender temporarily to the "automation" they have defied for so long, by accepting a tow from a powered boat. But only temporarily—they prefer mule or horse.

"We had Dolly destroyed a week ago," Mr. Skinner told "The Coventry Evening Telegraph," as he dipped a broom into the canal water and then brushed carefully over the gaily-painted woodwork of his boat.

"She was never the same," said his wife, "after she slipped into the canal in October, at a point where the towpath was in bad con-dition. That ducking did her no good.

"She rested for five weeks in the stables here, and then went back to work. But she was not like the same animal."

Mr. Skinner, who has worked on the canals since boyhood, could have had a boat with an engine long ago, but he preferred Dolly.

And because he owns his own boat he was able to keep her at a time when nationalised boats, and those owned by private com-panies, are all engine-powered. Mules and horses have disap-peared from the towpaths.

Coventry-built

Now Mr. Skinner and his wife Rose, who is Coventry-born, hope to maintain the tradition by obtaining another mule or horse.

They have had their boat Friendship for 30 years. It was built locally.

Today it remained at the canal side in Longford's quaint inland harbour as other working boats, of 54 which tied up at the stop for Christmas, were beginning to leave.

Some still carried their sprigs of holly and mistletoe as a reminder of family reunion parties during the holiday.

Power Station Party

One of the main gatherings for the boat families was a party for about 60 children.

The youngsters were taken on a special boat from Sutton Stop to the Longford Power Station of the Central Electricity Authority, to which many of the boats take coal, when the canteen had been made available for the party by Mr. R. W. Harvey, station superintendent.

The party was organised by Major F. Fielding, who is in charge of the Salvation Army boat at Sutton Stop.

Joe Skinner with his dog

Figure 19: A newspaper article about the death of 'Dolly' the mule

Figure 20: Dolly the mule pulling NB Friendship. Note the aluminium works in the background

Joe's nephew, Jack (John) Skinner chose a different means of working the canals. In 1946 he married Rose Hone (another well-known canal family) and began his married life on a motor boat called, *Kent* and a butty, *Forget Me Not*. They too moved various cargoes, but mostly coal from the Midlands to Oxford. They had four children who would accompany them on their travels. Rose conjures a vivid picture of life aboard,

'We used to eat as we went along – and I used to cook as we went along an' all! Cooking with one hand and steering with another. And the little ones playing in the boat's bottom when it was empty or tied to the slide [hatch] when we were loaded.' (source Davies/Robinson)

Although Jack and Rose couldn't read or write, they were excellent story tellers and had a wealth of knowledge about life on the canals. In their commendable book, Our Canal in Oxford (Towpath Press 1999), Mark Davies and Catherine Robinson chronicle their meeting the Skinners, with an extraordinary tale.

During World War II, Jack even transported a top-priority supply of nitroglycerine, which he and his mate delivered from Brentford to Birmingham up the Grand Union Canal through 153 locks,

'We did it in 63 hours, without stopping, kept going through the night, with a paraffin lamp on the front of the boat. That put years on me, that did! When we got to the other end, there were chaps all dressed in green fireproof stuff, with gloves and helmets. They said there was enough in one of those bottles to blow up Birnigum [sic] with!'

By 1963, the Skinners had moved to a cottage on the canal bank at Kidlington. Their proximity to the canal allowed them to continue to have an active part in waterways life. In 1967, Treasury officials had recommended filling in the canal, arguing that it was no longer commercially viable. Like Tom Rolt decades earlier, Jack Skinner was appalled by the idea. Tasked to take Barbara Castle, then minister of transport, on a fact-finding trip from Thrupp to Lower Heyford, he hatched a plan. He went out the night before and getting the cooperation of the lock keepers en-route, he made sure there would be enough water in the pounds to give the impression that navigation was far easier in the near-derelict canal than it actually was. "She never knew the difference - and it done the trick," he recalled years later. In April 2008, Jack died aged 88.

I was lucky enough to know Rose Skinner. She would frequently visit Banbury, usually on a Thursday as it's a market day. She regularly popped into the yard for a chat and to drop off photos that she thought that I would be interested in. I loved her visits and regarded her as canal royalty.

On the surface, she was quite unassuming, with the appearance of a typical storybook 'grandmother'. Regarding her as a harmless old woman, quietly seeing out her twilight years, was a mistake many who met her would make. Her deceptive appearance belied her previous life as an accomplished boatwoman from a long line of famous boaters. On more than one occasion, I chuckled to myself when boaters would laboriously, and with more than a hint of condescension, tell this little-old-lady all about life on the canal. If only they knew who they were talking to.

She had a keen sense of humour and would enjoy pulling my leg or having a laugh with me, or even at my expense. She didn't hesitate to voice her opinion and wouldn't hold back if she thought there was a better way of doing things. When we launched the *Dancing Duck* sideways into the canal, Rose could be heard on the other side of the water shouting that we were, "doing it all wrong."

Figure 21: Launching NB Dancing Duck built at Tooley's in 2007

On Saturday 24th April 2010, for the centenary of Tom Rolt's birth, there was a re-enactment of the original *Cressy* Cruise. It was organised and undertaken by the Inland Waterways Association (IWA) Oxfordshire Branch Chairman, Ron Heritage supported by his wife Mary on their narrowboat *Heron*. I was privileged to be at the helm of the *Dancing Duck*, heading the flotilla of boats which led *Heron* out of Banbury.

Even more remarkable, were the esteemed passengers I had on board the *Duck*, none other than, Rose Skinner and Sonia Rolt. Once we had waved Ron and Mary off, we headed back to Tooley's. Although it felt a little surreal to have both of these remarkable women on the last and most recent boat to be built and launched at Tooley's, the historical connection between each of us was undeniable. As I pondered this thought, I couldn't resist asking Rose if she fancied a steer? Despite being 85 years old, she jumped at the chance and confidently took the tiller. I knew we were in the safest of hands. Two years later, in June 2012 at the age of 87 Rose died. It was a privilege to have been her friend and to have been at the tiller with such a spirited and incredible woman.

Figure 22: NB Friendship moored at the towpath

Powered Boating

During the early developments of the steam engine, some were introduced to narrowboats. Boatyards therefore had to master new skills to repair and service the new technology. These bulky and heavy engines were far from practical to use on this type of craft. They needed to carry coal as fuel and water to create the steam. They also required an extra crew member to maintain them. On a boat designed to carry as much as possible – it all took up too much space to seem worth it. Note the space needed for the three man crew and the engine on this early steam narrowboat on the River Thames. (Below) Early steam trials on the canals in Scotland fared no better,

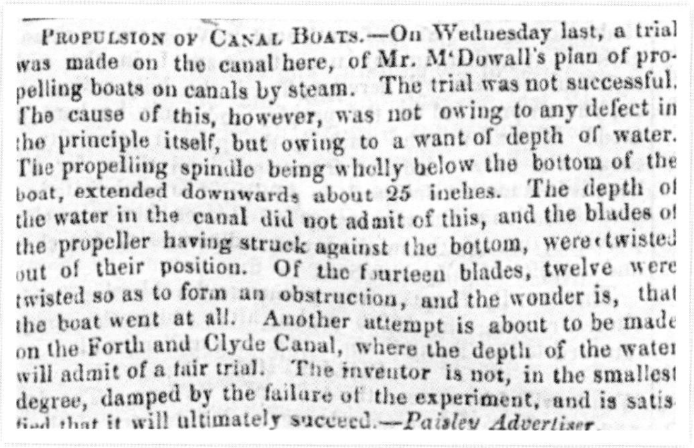

'Propulsion of Canal boats. – On Wednesday last, a trial was made on the canal here, of Mr. McDowall's plan of propelling boats on canals by steam. The trial was not successful. The cause of this, however, was not owing to any defect in the principle itself, but owing to a want of depth of water. The propelling spindle being wholly below the bottom of the boat, extended downwards about 25 inches. The depth of the water in the canal did not admit of this, and the blades of the propeller having struck against the bottom, were twisted out of their position. Of the fourteen blades, twelve were twisted so as to form an obstruction, and the wonder is, that the boat went at all. Another attempt is about to be made on the Forth and Clyde Canal, where the depth of the water will admit of a fair trial. The inventor is not, in the smallest degree, damped by the failure of the experiment, and is satisfied that it will ultimately succeed.' The Paisley Advertiser July 1840

PROPULSION OF CANAL BOATS.—On Wednesday last, a trial was made on the canal here, of Mr. M'Dowall's plan of propelling boats on canals by steam. The trial was not successful. The cause of this, however, was not owing to any defect in the principle itself, but owing to a want of depth of water. The propelling spindle being wholly below the bottom of the boat, extended downwards about 25 inches. The depth of the water in the canal did not admit of this, and the blades of the propeller having struck against the bottom, were twisted out of their position. Of the fourteen blades, twelve were twisted so as to form an obstruction, and the wonder is, that the boat went at all. Another attempt is about to be made on the Forth and Clyde Canal, where the depth of the water will admit of a fair trial. The inventor is not, in the smallest degree, damped by the failure of the experiment, and is satisfied that it will ultimately succeed.—*Paisley Advertiser*.

Figure 23: A newspaper cutting of steam boat trials in 1840

Figure 24: A steam narrowboat on the River Thames c.1910 (note the 3 man crew)

The advent of the diesel engine introduced in the early 1900s brought the most radical and significant change to the way narrowboats were powered. The reliable Bolinder diesel engine was introduced to great acclaim. Once again, boatyards learned new skills to fit, service and repair these emerging, and enduring types of boat engines.

The Great Depression saw a reduction in demand for new boats, but Tooley's Boatyard was able to survive by maintaining the many existing craft that continued to use the canal network. By 1939, when Rolt came to the yard to have *Cressy* fitted out, he observed,

'Time was when they built the long wooden boats at Tooley's yard, but now owing to the decline of canal traffic and the introduction of the steel boat, their work was confined to repairs. The average wooden narrow boat requires docking about once every three years, so that this work was spasmodic and, despite the fact that the family were prepared to tackle any job in the way of joinery or wheelwrighting that would tide them over, there were times when the yard fell slack.'

The introduction of the new diesel engines came with a distinct bonus. The greater power in the motor allowed an extra boat to be towed behind. Boats would work in pairs with the 'motor boat' doing the work and the unpowered 'butty' being pulled behind. In the 1930s over 300 such working boats were built by the Grand Union Canal Company.

Since the late 1800s, the railways had been taking large quantities of goods and materials and delivering them throughout the country. There was a problem however; unlike canalside wharfs, rail cargo would have to be transported to the railway goods yard itself, loaded on, then taken to another yard for unloading. Often, it would need further transportation to its final destination. By contrast, transport by boat was very slow. It takes fourteen hours from Banbury to Oxford by canal, even though it's only twenty-five miles away. Despite this, the end to end journey for cargo could sometimes be quicker than the railways. This was because canal boats were often loaded directly from factories and the cargo delivered to their intended wharfs and docks without the need for onward movement.

Moreover, many towns and emerging cities had grown up around their canals and rivers allowing freight and goods to be offloaded in their bustling centres. By contrast, railways would often be forced to the outskirts necessitating further journeys to their final destination.

In order to compete with the railways, the canal companies offered their services as cheaply as possible. They had to keep their costs down as much as practicable and it was said that neither the Tooleys nor their predecessors made any major capital investment in the buildings or their equipment. Although the Tooleys installed a Petter Oil engine in the machine shop, their policy was to make do and mend, spending as little as possible on the boatyard itself.

Before the Second World War, some working boats started to be converted to houseboats. They were known as 'pleasure boats' by the working boatman. In the same Waterways World article mentioned above, Herbert Tooley recalls that George senior was one of the pioneers of this development, converting horse boat, *Fair Trader* into a motor boat. Whilst rare, they began to appear in increasing numbers on the waterways. Nevertheless, the canals at this time were regarded as being old and obsolete, as their use continued to decline. They were badly maintained, if at all, and many were full of weeds and falling apart. To the working boatmen, the canal was a world of toil and transport, they considered it strange to regard it as a place where people would want to spend their leisure time.

The steady decline of the canal system after the Second World War, would arguably have seen most of the network disappear and sink back into the countryside it had so elegantly emerged from, but for the growth of the pleasure boat business. To many, the turning point can be traced directly to L T C

Rolt's publication of 'Narrow Boat' and his impressive journey on *Cressy*, which led to the formation of the Inland Waterways Association (IWA). It is worth noting that there are now more operable and usable canals and waterways in the United Kingdom than there were in the 1950s and 1960s. (source CRT) Moreover, there continues to be a healthy growth in restoration projects throughout the country, with communities and associations benefitting from the re-opening of once forgotten and abandoned stretches of water.

When Rolt had *Cressy* fitted out at Tooley's in 1939, the artisans and workers regarded the fitting of such 'luxuries' as a bath, toilet and sleeping quarters with incredulity,

'In the homes of the poor a fitted bath is still a rare luxury…on a canal boat it was… as fabulous as the swimming-pool of a millionaire. It was not surprising… that [its] arrival, should cause something of a stir in the boatyard.'

Figure 25: The newly fitted kitchen and bathroom on Cressy

Figure 26: Interior of L T C Rolt's motor Cressy

And yet the irony of 'luxury' wasn't lost on Rolt when he observed the love and care taken over the decoration of the boats themselves, when utility appeared more 'sensible'. After watching the elaborate decoration and painting of the narrowboat *Florence* he remarked,

'A modern economist would have pointed out quite truthfully that she would have been just as serviceable had she been painted battleship grey...'

But the skills of the Tooleys had dazzled him and he was determined to be part of the old traditions. Although this subject is covered in more detail later, it is helpful at this point to note his determination to utilise the Tooleys' talents,

'I obtained a promise from him [George Tooley Senior] that, when my own work on 'Cressy' had reached the decorating stage, he would paint for me a bunch of roses on each of the four panels in the sleeping cabin.'

These days, very few narrowboats are without 'luxuries' and their colour and pageantry form a huge part of the vibrancy and life of the waterways, many harking back to the styles and look of the original working boats. There are many annual shows and gatherings held around the waterways of Britain, where narrowboat owners take the opportunity to show off their pride and joy. What had previously been regarded as a niche pastime reserved only for dedicated, usually bearded enthusiasts of a certain age, has exploded into the wider public arena. Banbury Canal Day, celebrated on the first Sunday of October since 2004, now sees visitors in excess of 10,000 regularly attending. These gala days date back to 1995 and 1996 when the first Tooley's Open Days were held to raise awareness of the boatyard.

Figure 27: Tooley's Open Day 1990s

Figure 28: The 1996 Canal Weekend Committee

This photograph from 1996, demonstrates the overwhelming dedication, affection and enthusiasm for the canal in Banbury, but Tooley's Boatyard in particular. It is important to acknowledge here, that the efforts of everyone involved in these events during the 1990s was critical to the future safeguarding and development of Tooley's. It was the forerunner to the much celebrated and hugely successful, Banbury Canal Days, held every October.

It would not be unreasonable to conclude that the humble narrowboat has become as iconic a symbol of Britishness as a red telephone box, British Bobby, or even the Houses of Parliament!

CHAPTER THREE

THE TOOLEYS

Figure 29: Brothers George and Herbert in the dock

The Tooley family were involved in boating for three generations. It all began with Emanuel Tooley who, according to Bletchingdon Parish Church records, was baptised in October 1828. Official Census records of 1841 and 1851 show Emanuel and his family engaged in agricultural work in the Bletchingdon area of Oxfordshire. As farming work became scarce, he turned to working on the canal. He became a 'Number 1' meaning that he owned his boats and worked independently. It was his own business, and this allowed him to operate distinctly from the large canal carrying companies, such as Fellows Morton & Clayton. In the main, he moved iron bars and moulding sand between Samuelson's agricultural machinery factory in Banbury, and the Midlands. By the age of 45, he was recorded as the master of two boats, *Speedwell* and *Elizabeth*. (1881 Census)

In 1869 his son, George was born, in Banbury, Oxfordshire and he followed his father into working on the boats. Around 1901, George Tooley is believed to have leased the 'Banbury Boatyard' from the Oxford Canal Company. The boatyard at this time consisted of a stable, a forge, a dry dock, a boiler and steam chest.

George had no formal training in dock work; in fact, he had never worked in a dock before. Nevertheless, he learned quickly, had a keen eye and had often watched boat builders repairing his father's boats. He picked up many new skills as he progressed through the years. As the business became more established, his father joined him working in the dock, although it was always seen as George's business. Emanuel Tooley continued to keep a keen eye on the business throughout his later years. He died in 1917 at the age of 89 and is buried at St. Mary's Church, Banbury.

George became very skilled, and the Tooleys soon established their boatyard as a significant business within the canal system. George was the epitome of the self-made businessman. He was often seen working with his shirt sleeves rolled up, with a waistcoat and the essential status symbol, a bowler hat. George had two sons, George Junior born in 1903, and Herbert born in 1913. Their father ensured the future of the yard by teaching the boys all the skills necessary for working in the boatyard.

Crucial to their success was their sustained boating trade on the canal. Although they had the dock, they continued to take loads to and from

Samuelson's, by employing boatmen to do it for them. In this way, they always understood what their customers at the yard needed, helping to build and establish trust within the boating community. Later, when they stopped moving loads, their former working vessels became exchange boats for the dock. This was not the end of the family's connection with cargo deliveries, however. George senior had an older brother, Will, who traded on the River Nene as a coal merchant, where he and his family delivered coal from Warwickshire.

When George Tooley took on the yard, there was no cover over the dock. It was open to the elements, and therefore work was completed outside in all weathers. At that time, there was only one building on the site, the forge, which was built at the same time as the dock, or very close to it. There had originally been four workshops, but these were destroyed when a pitch boiler caught fire and burnt down in 1897.

This dramatic incident was chronicled by the Banbury Guardian. They reported that on 25th November 1897 the Banbury Fire Brigade was called out to a fire at Neal's dockyard in Factory Street. When they got there, they found that four buildings on the site were "a mass of flames". The fire hydrant in Factory Street would not work and they had problems putting out the flames. They were worried about the fire spreading to other buildings, one of which was rumoured to contain gunpowder. So, Captain Fortescue sent a message for the steam powered fire engine – the Steamer Victoria, to attend and put out the fire.

Figure 30: Banbury Steam Fire Engine circa 1910

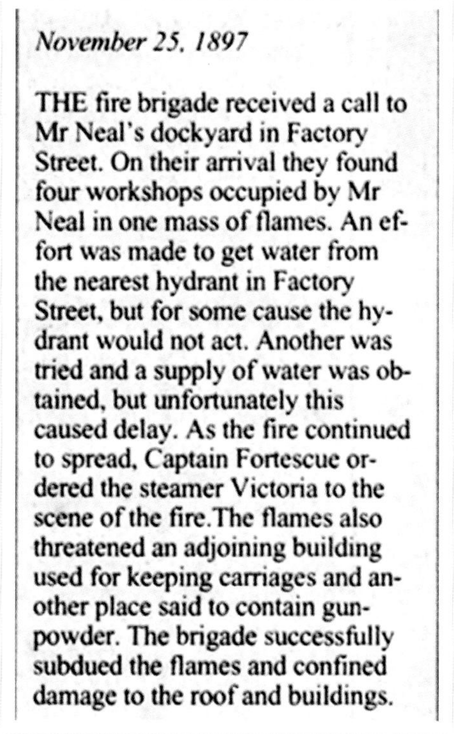

November 25, 1897

THE fire brigade received a call to Mr Neal's dockyard in Factory Street. On their arrival they found four workshops occupied by Mr Neal in one mass of flames. An effort was made to get water from the nearest hydrant in Factory Street, but for some cause the hydrant would not act. Another was tried and a supply of water was obtained, but unfortunately this caused delay. As the fire continued to spread, Captain Fortescue ordered the steamer Victoria to the scene of the fire.The flames also threatened an adjoining building used for keeping carriages and another place said to contain gunpowder. The brigade successfully subdued the flames and confined damage to the roof and buildings.

Figure 31: Newspaper cutting of the fire at 'Neal's Boatyard' 1897

Ironically, it may have been this event which allowed George Tooley to afford to take on the yard. Recovery from a major fire would have been difficult and challenging at that time. The loss of four buildings was also likely to affect the value of the business.

New opportunities were emerging and from 1907 until 1929, George looked after and docked the local Kirtlington based Oxford & Portland Cement Company's working fleet of boats. They had six boats, and the Tooleys are known to have built two of them. These vessels had the reputation of being kept in immaculate condition and they were a credit to the Tooleys. The cement works at what is locally known as 'The Quarry' no longer survives, but the remnants of the site can still be clearly seen. When this cement works closed in 1929 a new one opened up a short distance south at Shipton-on-Cherwell and is still working to this day. It's easy to spot contemporary boaters who have recently negotiated this River Cherwell section of the Oxford Canal; they emerge as ghosts of the cut, covered as they are in a thick layer of cement dust!

The Tooleys were particularly adept when it came to working on wooden boats. There are many accounts of their skills and proficiency with wood at the boatyard. In a 1982 Waterways World article, Herbert Tooley recalls that his father built twelve such boats between 1900 and 1928 and went on to describe the process in detail. He said it took about six months to build a wooden boat. They were all built outside the dock in the open. Elm wood was used as a bottom plank across a frame for the base. Then the keelson, a 4ins x 9ins (10 x 23cm) section of oak, was laid down the centre, running the full length of the vessel. The keelson was made in three sections and was secured by spikes being driven through the bottom planks into the keelson itself. He described how they kept and reused old iron 'knees'. The knees were large 'L' brackets which were bolted to the bottom planks, which in turn, allowed the side oak planks to be bolted on to them. The joints were then caulked to make them watertight. The stem and stern posts were also made from solid oak. The end curved planks were steamed to soften them and held in place with clamps. Any shaping of the wood was done by hand with adzes and saws.

Figure 32: Jim Mobbs at the controls of his engine, making steam for planking

Figure 33: A wooden boat showing its 'knees' in the dock

It all took place on the canal side, which was essential as once complete they would be broadside launched by sliding them sideways into the canal. From there they were floated into the dry dock to be finished off.

Figure 34: The launch of NB Savannah at Tooley's Boatyard 1913

This craftsmanship had a long and noble history throughout the country, whether in seafaring yards or inland. It was recognised that such skills took years to perfect, providing status and due recognition from fellow artisans and boaters alike. A connection with the land and nature was essential in the understanding of boatbuilding. A practical example of this connection is referred to by Tom Rolt in 'Narrow Boat',

'The craftsman's solution is to obtain a timber having one correct curve already in the grain… Mr. Tooley… related how, years ago, he had spotted a suitable oak tree on the outskirts of the town and…when it was to be felled…he bought it. Now it lay in the yard sawn into timbers ready for use…'

Herbert and George Junior had been working at the boatyard since the 1920s. They had worked under the close supervision of their father, developing the skills necessary to build, repair and maintain boats. When they were old enough they would help out at the boatyard after school and at weekends. By 1939, they were renowned for their expertise and artistry, which is why Tom Rolt chose to have his now legendary narrowboat, *Cressy*, fitted out at the yard. This critical meeting is covered in more detail later, but it was to prove vital to the post war success of the canal and waterways network.

One year into the Second World War, in 1940, George Tooley senior died aged 71. He'd been ill for some months and had a period of hospitalisation for pneumonia, from which he never fully recovered. He would have been aware of the revival of the canals due to the war effort, and the need for Tooley's to play its part. It was during these uncertain and troubled times that Herbert took over the business, with help from his brother George. Goods, munitions, weapons and other vital items were regularly moved by boat during the conflict. The traffic on canals increased and boats needed repairs and maintenance. Tooley's yard and skills were in demand and their vital contribution to keeping the canals as an effective part of Britain's wartime effort was critical in securing victory over Nazi Germany. Finding and retaining a sufficiently skilled workforce was challenging to all industries, but it was particularly acute on the waterways. Indeed, George Tooley had to make a court application to retain some of his staff as seen in this newspaper extract. The person named in this article is Ernest Carvell, who as we shall see later was a renowned and highly skilled, canal boat artist.

Mr. E. L. Fisher appeared in support of an application by Mr. George Tooley, canal barge repairer and builder, Factory Street, Banbury, for the exemption of Ernest Albert Carvell, of the Causeway, Grimsbury, in his employ as barge maker and repairer.—Mr. Tooley, in answer to Mr. Fisher, said he was the only boat builder and repairer in Banbury, and the nearest man in the trade was at Braunston, near Daventry. He usually employed three men before the war, besides working himself. One of those men was now serving in France, and the other was at the munition works. Carvell was the only man left in his employ, and he could not do without him. Witness usually repaired eight or ten boats a year, and sometimes built new barges. He had the repairing of three boats on hand at the present time. Carvell did the painting as well as general work, and an ordinary carpenter would not be able to do the work. Without Carvell he could not carry on the business.—Mr. Fisher produced Carvell's medical card, showing he had been passed for labour at home.—The Chairman said the Local Tribunal thought that Carvell should be exempted till his employer had completed the work he had on hand. How long would it take to do that?—Appellant said about a month, but he wanted to know what was his position before taking on the building of a new boat and laying out his money.—The Chairman: The answer to that is " Don't start on the building of a new boat."—Appellant said he could not get another man in Carvell's place.—The Tribunal dismissed the appeal, with leave to make further application to the Borough Tribunal.

Figure 35: George Tooley applies for an exemption for Ernest Carvell

Figure 36: Heather Wastie of Alarum Theatre wearing an IW badge

Due to the acute shortage of labour, women were called upon to play a vital role within the canal network. As in other fundamental professions, many boatmen had been called up to fight, leaving their boats and families behind. All over the country, women from mainly middle-class backgrounds could be seen at the tiller of working boats throughout the waterways network. They had been recruited from across the country to work in areas traditionally occupied by men. Training was tough and arduous and not all recruits were able to finish the course of instruction. The goal was to earn the coveted IW (Inland Waterways) badge shown below. In fact, these badges were only issued after 1944 and were given to men as well as women. Jack Skinner, referred to earlier, was known to have owned one. Many of us involved in waterways history are aware of the egregious nickname, 'Idle Women', that these volunteer boat women had apparently earned. It had been assumed, and has often been repeated, that this was a common term used throughout the war to describe the female skippers and crews of the working boats. I'm grateful to Kate Saffin and Heather Wastie of the Alarum Theatre Company for illuminating the facts behind this myth. The name 'Idle Women' is the title of Susan Woolfitt's 1947 book which chronicles the lives of these remarkable boatwomen during the war. The title was, in fact, suggested by Woolfitt's daughter, Harriet and was never used by, or about these tough and resolute volunteers.

Although Banbury didn't suffer the horrendous fate of places like London, Coventry, Portsmouth and many other towns and cities, it did receive attention from the Luftwaffe. The nearby railway sidings took a direct hit in 1940, killing six local men. More ominously, that same year saw two bombs targeted on the main canal lock a short distance away from Tooley's Boatyard. Joyce Beasley records the bombing in her as yet unpublished biography of her husband's time on narrowboats, in 'The Boy Off the Boats'. The night before the raid the Beasley family decided to leave the town, mooring up their working boats at nearby Twyford Bridge. It turned out to be a very wise decision,

'The next morning a lengthsman came and told them that Banbury lock had been bombed in the night, if they'd stayed there they would have been a gonner. A 500 pounder in the lock and another in the basin. Nobody was killed thank the Lord. George [Beasley] was relieved to hear that the 'Strugglers Inn' was

still standing, even though it had been rocked on its feet. The only real casualty had been Mrs Malloy's cockerel, he'd lost every single feather but he was still crowing, and Mrs Malloy was already charging '6d a look' for the Spitfire fund.'

Although damaged, the gates of the lock fortunately held fast, or the town may well have been flooded. Nevertheless, it was a very close shave for the town and for Tooley's in particular. Joyce Beasley goes on to describe the effect this had on local trade,

'After the lock was bombed, and while Mr Bloomfield and his gang of maintenance men rebuilt it, they had to unload at Castle Street Wharf straight on to the Co-op's own horse and carts. The Co-op had their own coal lorries, but they used horse and carts in the wartime to save petrol.'

To this day, the repair block bearing the year 1940 can clearly be seen in lock number 29 in Banbury town centre (shown below).

Figure 37: '1940' clearly marked when the Banbury lock was repaired

Figure 38: The devastation left following the bombing of Banbury lock in 1940

The years after the war were particularly challenging for the canal network. Demand on the canals and waterways generally fell dramatically and work became more difficult, as more goods were moved by rail and road. Large fleets of surplus army trucks were purchased to form many new haulage companies. Traditional Number 1s were in decline as the lure of more lucrative work on the roads beckoned. Water traffic slowed, whilst the movement of goods by road and rail increased. Work in the boatyard began a steady decline.

There wasn't enough to keep both Tooleys fully occupied. Herbert continued at the boatyard, while George went on to find alternative employment in a local aluminium factory. However, George was regularly on hand to help his brother with some of the trickier tasks such as planking. It was this stark decline of the waterways, that Tom Rolt witnessed so acutely and fought so hard to reverse.

Pete Downer has been part of the fabric of the canals around Banbury for over forty years. His knowledge and skills within the boating community of the Oxford Canal are renowned. He still runs Banbury Boatyard Services to this day and remembers George and Herbert with affection. Often seen at the

Figure 39: Herbert Tooley applying detailing at the bow of a narrowboat

yard, helping out or working on his own unique projects, he has many
memories and anecdotes of the Tooley brothers, working arrangements.
One such occasion was when George and Herbert were working together
putting some planks in the side of a narrowboat. They were arguing and
bickering with each other throughout the process. Herbert suddenly noticed
the time and announced, "Tea anyone?" After a short disappearance,
he emerged with a tray laden with cups of tea and biscuits. All previous
arguments and annoyances were forgotten, and the moment was lightened
with laughter and joshing. Tea break over, it's back to work and they pick
up their tools, and with them, their earlier argument!

Figure 40: George and Herbert Tooley caulking in the dock

Figure 41: A young Pete Downer working on a gearbox

Despite the reduced demand, the yard somehow managed to survive through the lean years up until the 1980s. The family home had been at 11 Factory Street in Banbury, but by the 1960s the town was undergoing regeneration and the property was compulsorily purchased and demolished. Herbert initially rented a boat at the yard, but later bought a caravan which he located next to the dock. He lived in this small space for the next twenty-five years. A proposal to develop the area around Tooley's into a marina with offices and a glass fronted showroom left Herbert baffled. The plans had proposals to dispose of the original dock and replace it with a new, shorter forty feet long version. He had to remind the developers about the length of most of the craft on canals being well over forty feet, with very many being around seventy feet. Following a huge campaign to save the yard by boaters and locals alike, the proposal for the development was defeated. In 1974, Cherwell District Council recognised the historical importance of Tooley's and following their application to the Department of the Environment a Preservation Order was placed on the boatyard.

Living in the caravan was difficult for Herbert. He'd suffered from polio and walked with a limp, making getting around difficult. As he grew older the work on the boats became more challenging. He managed to supplement his meagre income with a connection to the famous Hoods ironmongers in Banbury town centre. He would receive various tools to be sharpened and lawnmowers and other mechanical objects for mending. In the forge, Jack Plester would burn out tool handles for the ironmonger so that new ones could replace them. Herbert and Jack would also work together to provide a wheelwrighting service for Hoods customers.

Figure 42: The boatyard in the mid 1980s showing Herbert's caravan

The enduring relationship between Pete Downer and Herbert was critical to the continued existence of the historical yard. A 'gentlemen's' agreement was struck between the two, whereby Pete would rent out the dock and lend an occasional hand to Herbert for the irregular boat work that he continued to take on. Pete recalls the last boat that Herbert worked on was a wooden narrowboat named, *Clara*. It was famously in the dock for seven years in total! *Clara* is still afloat can still be seen around the waterways of England.

Figure 43: NB Clara outside the dock

In May 1987, Herbert Tooley died at the age of 73. This unassuming, frail and slight man passed away in the place he had been so close to throughout his life. It seemed fitting and appropriate that he would forever be at the heart of the yard that would evermore bear his family name. His obituary in the August 1987 edition of Waterways World summed up his life perfectly,

'With his passing we have lost a quiet, genuine English Craftsman, a staunch friend of the canals and of many of their users, and one who imparted to the Oxford Canal much of its character.'

The future of the yard was far from certain following Herbert's passing. British Waterways agreed to let Pete Downer use the dock and yard on a temporary basis until 1988, following a meeting with officials and Herbert's brother George. George had not been actively involved with the yard for some time and as he was now in his eighties, couldn't be expected to continue the business. A new leaseholder was found, and Barrie Morse ran Morse Marine from 1990 to 1998 from the yard. Pete Downer continued to hire the dock occasionally during this time.

Herbert Tooley

Yet another link with waterway history has been severed with the death, on 5th June last, of Herbert Tooley of Banbury.

Tooley's Boatyard at Banbury must be the best and least known boatyard on the entire system. Best, because it was here, in 1939, that L. T. C. Rolt, fitted out his ex Shroppie fly boat *Cressy* and the yard became immortalised in the pages of *Narrow Boat*. Least, because Herbert Tooley was a shy, diffident craftsman of the old school, who abhored publicity and razzmatazz, who only asked that he should be left alone to earn his living in his own way.

Herbert's father George, as described by Rolt, was a boatman, turned-boatbuilder, who took over the small dockyard above Banbury lock sometime about the end of the Great War, and his two sons joined him in the enterprise.

Following the death of his father, Herbert continued the yard's existence by turning out small quantities of high quality work; one of his last regular commercial customers was the late Joe Skinner whose *Friendship* now preserved at Ellesmere Port, was most splendidly repainted at Banbury in 1958 or thereabouts.

In later years Herbert Tooley endured much bureaucratic persecution from tidy-minded officials who wished to see a more "appropriate" development in Banbury town centre (such as the loathesome bus station, built on the old canal basin), but frail and slight as he appeared he saw them and their schemes off the premises.

With his passing we have lost a quiet, genuine English Craftsman, a staunch friend of the canals and of many of their users, and one who imparted to the Oxford Canal much of its character.

It will be a sad day for the waterways, and for the people of Banbury, if the bureaucrats finally succeed in obliterating the yard where so much of our modern waterway history began.

David Blagrove

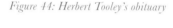

Figure 44: Herbert Tooley's obituary

Figure 45: Herbert Tooley

In October 1993 George Tooley died at the age of 88 following a short illness. This closed the final chapter of almost a century of association with the yard. Yet, the family's legacy continues to this day and whilst the yard still operates it will always simply be known as 'Tooleys'.

Figure 46: Morse Marine open day 1990s

George Henry Tooley

OBITUARY

ONE of Banbury's finest craftsmen has died at the age of 88.

George Henry Tooley, son of George Tooley the boat builder, died at Banbury's Horton Hospital on October 26 after a short illness.

Mr Tooley was born on December 21, 1904 at Southam. He moved to Factory Street in Banbury with his family when he was very young.

Mr Tooley worked in the boatyard and learned his craft under the expert eye of his father until 1934 when the boat trade slumped and he went to work at Northern Aluminium Company, now Alcan. But after his shifts at the factory, he would return to the boatyard to continue work with his father and brother, Herbert.

Arthur Jones, from Banbury's East Close, attended the National School with Mr Tooley. He remembers the vicar, Canon Jones, bestowing on Mr Tooley the fitting nickname of Sage Tooley. Mr Jones recalls George Tooley's skills in the use of long-forgotten tools of wrought iron-making, caulking irons, timber sawing and bending and well as the traditional narrow boat painting and sign writing.

Mr Tooley was a shy, quiet man with a keen interest in pho-

■ George Henry Tooley.

tography and all things mechanical. He was a chorister at St Mary's Church for 80 years and was presented with a special chorister's medal after 75 years.

Mr Tooley married Margaret in 1946. She died in 1991.

Mr Tooley's enduring links with St Mary's were celebrated at his funeral service conducted by the Rev Andrew Duff on Monday when past as well as present members of the choir sang. The service was followed by cremation at Oakley Wood.

Figures 47: George Tooley's obituary

Figure 48: George Tooley looking at the engine of NB Clara. Herbert Tooley in the background

CHAPTER FOUR

TOM ROLT

Figure 49: Tom Rolt on NB Cressy

To many boaters and waterways enthusiasts, Tom, or L T C Rolt, is regarded as the saviour of many, if not most of the modern-day canals. His seminal work, Narrow Boat, referred to throughout this book, was published in 1944. It was a huge success. He chronicled his journey through a way of life which was clearly and immediately threatened. At the unveiling of Rolt's blue plaque in August 2010, the Oxford historian Mark Davies asserted in a BBC interview,

'It's probably the most important book about the inland waterways ever written…' (source BBC Radio Oxford)

Figure 50: Tom Rolt's blue plaque

Rolt's determination and campaigning to rescue the canals from an uncertain future led to the formation of the Inland Waterways Association (IWA) in 1946. The efforts of the IWA led to a distinct change in attitude from government policy makers and bureaucrats. The threat of wholesale closure and termination of the canals receded, although their long-term fate between the 1950s and 1980s remained precarious. As we now know from his account in Narrow Boat, Rolt also had great affection for the Banbury Boatyard, and the Tooleys in particular, all of whom he'd met during his stay in 1939.

Lionel Thomas Caswell Rolt was born in Chester on 11th February 1910 during the rise of the railway mania, and the slow decline of the canals. He attended Cheltenham College until he left, aged 16 years, to take up an apprenticeship at Kerr Stuart Locomotive Works in Stoke-on-Trent, where his uncle, Kyrle Willans, was chief development engineer. This was a very fortunate turn of events as it was Kyrle who introduced Tom to the pleasures of boating. He owned the narrowboat butty, *Cressy*, a name now etched into the annals of narrowboat history. It was originally intended to be horse-drawn and had a traditional wooden hull with no engine. They initially fitted it with a steam engine, but soon realised that steam wasn't the ideal mechanism for a narrowboat, especially in tunnels. Using their engineering skills, they later replaced it with a Ford Model T engine.

The depression of the 1930s saw the end of Rolt's career in steam. Nevertheless, his passion for engineering continued in the form of motor cars, and he bought a part share of a garage in Hampshire. It was while working in his garage he met his future wife, Angela Orred, who shared his passion for vintage cars. Their relationship blossomed with Angela taking a keen interest in his boating exploits. At this time, cars were beginning to be mass produced, a development Rolt derided, which led to his change in career. He wanted to spend more time writing, was about to be married and he now needed to find a new home, so he sold off his part of the garage. With an uncertain future and dubious prospects, it is perhaps unsurprising that Angela's father didn't regard Rolt as 'son-in-law' material. However, the couple were determined to be together, despite any opposition; they married in secret on the 11th of July 1939.

An immediate problem for the newlyweds was where to live Rolt's brilliant idea was to approach his uncle Kyrle with an offer of £100 for the purchase of *Cressy*. At that time, the boat was far from habitable and needed a good deal of work to turn it into a comfortable home. It would take skill and time to transform this old wooden, 'Shroppie fly-boat' into a genuine pleasure boat, or 'live-aboard'. Tooley's Boatyard at Banbury was the ideal place for such a transformation. It was to become a place which Tom and Angela regarded with genuine wonder and fondness for many years ahead. It was, as we have seen in other parts of this book, Rolt's opportunity to chronicle his time on the waterways and develop his considerable writing skills.

Figure 51: Interior of L T C Rolt's motor Cressy with Angela Rolt

He developed a lasting friendship with the Tooleys. His detailed descriptions of them and the work done in the yard, are a particularly poignant aspect of his writing in Narrow Boat. He was fascinated with all aspects of the yard's work, most especially the painting and artwork. He was fortunate enough to observe all three Tooleys demonstrate their individual skills at close quarters during his time in Banbury in 1939. George junior was a renowned lettering expert. His father, George senior, would then embellish these letters with flowers and garlands. Herbert would then finish off the job with his personal take on the castles theme. Rolt's enthralment at this free-hand dexterity is evident as he depicts the scene perfectly,

'To behold him, (George snr) as I did, when he sat before the bench in his narrow workshop, the battered bowler firmly planted on the back of his head and a tray of many coloured paints at his elbow, was to see the past miraculously living in the present.'

Figure 52: George Tooley senior painting roses and castles in the paint shop

Rolt was determined to secure a piece of this 'miraculous past' on his own boat and persuaded an ailing George senior to embellish *Cressy* before he embarked on his journey through the canals. Unfortunately, old George Tooley had been taken seriously ill with pneumonia, requiring a period of hospitalisation. Nevertheless, he was a man of his word and, as soon as he was able, he returned to the yard to fulfil his promise. Each of the four panels of the sleeping cabin were decorated with a form of the Tooley rose. The moment was bitter sweet however, as he observed,

'The work tired him exceedingly, he rested frequently on the stool I provided for him but his hand was still sure. He has painted no flowers since.'

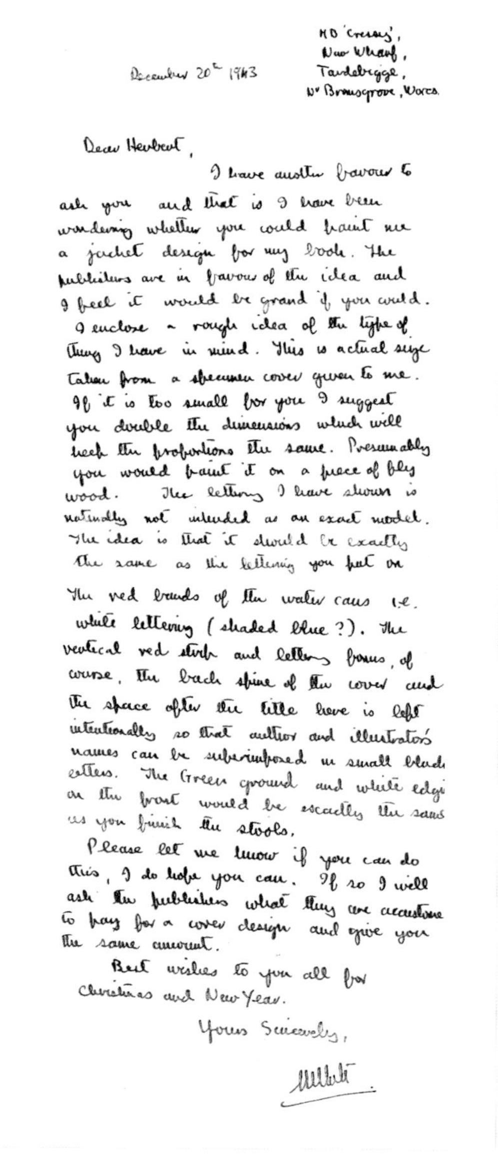

Figure 53: A letter from Tom Rolt to George Tooley requesting specialist painting

N.b. 'Cressy',
New Wharf,
Tardebigge,
Nr Bromsgrove, Worcs.

December 20ᵉ 1943

Dear Herbert,

I have another favour to ask you and that is I have been wondering whether you could paint me a jacket design for my book. The publishers are in favour of the idea and I feel it would be grand if you could. I enclose a rough idea of the type of thing I have in mind. This is actual size taken from a specimen cover given to me. If it is too small for you I suggest you double the dimensions which will keep the proportions the same. Presumably you would paint it on a piece of ply wood. The lettering I have shown is naturally not intended as an exact model. The idea is that it should be exactly the same as the lettering you put on the red bands of the water cans i.e. white lettering (shaded blue?). The vertical red strip and lettering forms, of course, the back spine of the cover and the space after the title here is left intentionally so that author and illustrator's names can be superimposed in small black letters. The Green ground and white edges on the front would be exactly the same as you finish the stools.

Please let me know if you can do this, I do hope you can. If so I will ask the publishers what they are accustomed to pay for a cover design and give you the same amount.

Best wishes to you all for Christmas and New Year.

Yours Sincerely,

Abbot.

Perhaps the biggest compliment and endorsement of Rolt's respect for the Tooleys was the use of Herbert Tooley's artwork in the form of roses, as the cover of the iconic book. Following the death of George Tooley senior in 1940, Rolt turned to Herbert for a 'favour' as shown in his hand-written letter dated December 1943. The original title for the book was 'Painted Ship', which was no doubt in recognition of the boat builder's artistic skill.

Figure 54: The cover of Rolt's Narrow Boat

Following the re-fit at Tooley's in July 1939, Tom and Angela embarked upon their four-month canal journey as recorded in Narrow Boat. The Second World War was to cut the trip short, with Tom's engineering skills being utilised at the Rolls-Royce factory at Crewe. Here, he could be found working on the Spitfire's Merlin engine production line, but he later worked at the Aldbourne foundry.

Figure 55: NB Cressy in Tooley's dry dock

Rolt submitted his waterways tale to various publishers without success. It wasn't until he wrote a magazine article extract that the book achieved the attention it deserved. In December 1944, it was first published under the new name 'Narrow Boat'.

It soon became a success with fan mail and supporting letters flooding in. Two of these letters were from Robert Aickman and Charles Hadfield. Tom invited Robert Aickman on a cruise on *Cressy* and it was here they discussed the future of the waterways. A plan was hatched and in May 1946 they formed the 'Inland Waterways Association'. They campaigned for the greater use of canals and rivers and to resist the deterioration and frequent abandonment of the underfunded and dilapidated canals. The positions within this new association were as follows: Chairman - Robert Aickman, Vice Chairman - Charles Hadfield and Secretary - Tom Rolt.

By 1948, the canals were nationalised and with public money in short supply they were immediately at risk. Post war austerity forced the new Labour government into making stark and often difficult decisions about all aspects of everyday life. The new welfare state and fledgling NHS forced policy makers to count every available penny. British Waterways was no exception, and one of their first cost-cutting proposals was to close the Stratford-upon-Avon Canal. This beautiful stretch of the network would certainly have been lost forever but for the campaign by the newly formed Inland Waterways Association. Their pressure and passion shone through, resulting in a celebrated reversal of its closure. This success was only one of many which were to see numerous communities fight alongside the IWA for their local waterways' survival.

Despite the obvious successes of the IWA, there were tensions within the organisation and in 1951, the IWA expelled Rolt as he had been prepared to compromise over partial canal closures. Robert Aickman wanted all waterways to be open and available for the carriage of cargo, something Rolt was reportedly sceptical about. By this time, Rolt's relationship with Angela was also under strain and she left him to join Billy Smart's circus as a ringmaster.

A few years earlier whilst at the IWA, Rolt had met Sonia Smith, a former actress and volunteer boat-woman. Interestingly, Sonia was the only IWA committee member with 'professional' cargo carrying experience. She had served as boatwoman volunteer during the war and was married to George Smith, an accomplished, although illiterate, boatman. By 1950, her marriage had broken down and she decided to leave the waterways. Turning their backs on canal life, Tom and Sonia left together to run the Talyllyn Railway in Mid Wales. After their respective divorces, Sonia and Tom married in 1952. They had two sons, Tim and Dick, and they eventually moved back to Rolt's family home in Stanley Pontlarge, near Cheltenham, where they lived until Tom Rolt's death in 1974 at the age of 64.

In later years, the rift with the IWA was healed when Sonia became more involved. She was awarded an OBE in 2011 for services to heritage and industrial archaeology. She died on 22 October 2014 at the age of 95. (Source: Guardian Obituary 31 Oct 2014) The IWA is a national organisation with a network of volunteers and branches. It is a registered charity and calls itself 'The Voice of the Waterways that advocates the conservation, use, maintenance, restoration and development of all inland waterways for public benefit'. It actively works to protect and restore the country's 6,500 miles of canals and rivers.

In July 1999, Cherwell District Council recognised the importance of Banbury's association with Tom Rolt and Tooley's Boatyard, when they unveiled the newly named Tom Rolt Bridge over the Oxford Canal and River Cherwell.

Figure 56: Tom Rolt's bridge plaque one

Figure 57: Tom Rolt's bridge plaque two

Not everyone involved with our contemporary waterways system has heard of Tooley's Boatyard or even L T C Rolt, but it is hard to deny that without their fortunate meeting in 1939, the current healthy state of Britain's canals and rivers could be very different indeed. Although Tom Rolt wrote many books and commented in various journals, his most memorable and influential work was undoubtedly Narrow Boat, which continues to influence and enthral readers to this day.

CHAPTER FIVE

THE BUILDINGS

Figure 58: Restaurant Boat Rosamund the Fair outside modern Tooley's

Dry Dock

Figure 59: A narrowboat, freshly painted and ready to leave the dock

The dry dock is the beating heart of Tooley's Boatyard. The chamber fills and empties with the lifeblood of the Oxford Canal every time a boat needs to be worked upon. It is 86ft (26m) long and 16ft 6ins (5m) wide, the water level on average varies from 2ft 6ins (0.8m) deep at the entrance to 4ft 6ins (1.4m) deep at the southern end. Whilst the world around it has changed beyond recognition, this dry dock continues to function exactly as it has done since 1778.

Its original purpose was to service horse drawn wooden narrowboats which were light and not very deep. The water level at the entrance to the dock is around 2ft (0.6m) which may not seem much, but it allows most craft access. Deeper draft boats, up to around 2ft 6ins (0.8m) or more can be accommodated, but these need to be winched in.

Figure 60: The dock re-filling after Banbury Canal Day

At the entrance is a cofferdam, consisting of three heavy wooden planks, which holds the water of the canal at bay. A cofferdam is a structure which holds back water, usually allowing work to be completed on its dry side. Construction material can vary from wood to clay, bricks or even concrete.

There are chocks securing the planks in place and when removed, the top plank can be lifted slightly, allowing water to rush into the dock. It takes a few minutes to fill and flood the whole of the inside. Once full, the planks are removed. Boats can then be brought inside on the water and tied off. The planks can then be repositioned and the water drained off through a sluice gate into a culvert. The dam is not entirely watertight, so the excess water is drained off in two drainage channels at either side of the dock. With the area inside now effectively 'dry', the boat is able to rest gently on iron girders or on the centuries old bricked floor.

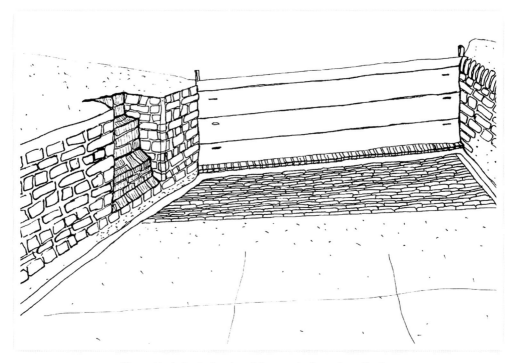

Figure 61: A simple drawing of the stop planks on the coffer dam

The traditional method to seal the planks was to use clay and ash. Once the planks were in place and slotted into the grooves in the ancient walls and held firmly in place with chocks, it was safe to pull the plug. As the water receded, clay was forced between the planks from the inside. Then ash was poured into the canal in front of the planks. Ash is ideal for this as is doesn't sink quickly and is briefly suspended in the water. If there are any leaks, then the ash is sucked into the holes and seals them. Particularly challenging and persistent leaks respond well to caulking.

This process may seem relatively simple, but it requires knowledge and understanding to become proficient in it. It was whilst I was running the Jericho Boatyard, that I obtained special permission to use the abandoned dry dock on the site. Our restaurant boat was docked there, and I used the old method of clay and ash to seal the planks. It only took me three days to achieve this! Today, at Tooley's, we use a large plastic tarpaulin as a seal. It works instantly, is completely reliable and is not as messy or time consuming as clay. However, we do occasionally call on the past to help out, reverting to 'ashing' if we have any leaks.

Figure 62: The author, Matt, with Jamie letting water into the dock

The culvert is an extremely important part of Tooley's dry dock. Not all dry docks have culverts, some have powered pumps. Anything which blocks or prevents the canal water from emptying, undermines the whole operation. The original fitting was 12ins x 12ins (0.3m x 0.3m) and made of elm. At the time of building the dockyard in 1778, the Oxford Canal only went as far south as Banbury. There was therefore, nowhere to drain the water away from the inside. The solution was to direct it around 394ft (120m) away to the Mill stream. This presented its own tricky challenges. In the 1980s the culvert was damaged while the canal was being dredged, causing water to rush back into the dock. The shocked workers were forced to scurry out as

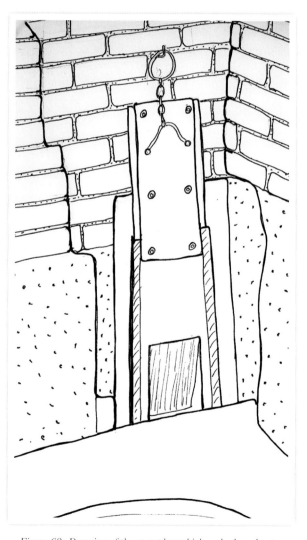

Figure 63: Drawing of the open plug which seals the culvert

the water poured back through the broken culvert. It was eventually repaired and replaced with a modern 6ins (0.15m) diameter pipe.

Canals collect all kinds of rubbish and sometimes it's washed into the dock. In order to prevent the culvert blocking up completely, there are four silt traps fitted along its length. These traps allow access and the ability to climb down to remove blockages, not the most popular or glamorous of tasks, although some of the items trapped here can be very interesting.

This system is really fragile and even a few twigs can cause items to catch and cause a blockage. To try and prevent this, the entrance to it has a series of wire meshes to try and catch items before they get sucked in and block everything up. The first trap is original and is made from old bricks; it resembles a well about 7ft (2m) deep. The other silt traps are modern and become progressively deeper as the water slopes off towards the river. It's not always clear where problems are located. This therefore, necessitates regular trips down each trap. Clearing them can only be done by manually digging out or using rods.

One memorable occasion was during an inspection of the fourth silt trap. This can be particularly tricky, due to the heavy foliage in the grounds of Chamberlin Court on the other side of the canal. I had removed the heavy cast iron manhole cover and found the trap full of water. By using rods, I managed to reduce the water level sufficiently to allow me to climb down a series of metal hand and foot holds. I was soon standing in 3ft (0.9m) of water at the bottom of a 12ft (3.6m) trap, in a pair of chest waders, wearing a head torch – not for the faint hearted! The bottom was full of silt, which was covering and blocking the exit pipe. The only way to fix the problem was to manually dig out the silt, put it into bucket loads and haul them to the surface on ropes. Gradually, I realised I was reaching the point where the culvert would be clear. I could hear and feel that things were beginning to ease, as I dislodged the last remnants of the obstruction. With a loud gurgle and froth of bubbles I was happy to be finishing a messy job. Suddenly, I realised I wasn't alone down there as a startled, but no doubt relieved 3ft (0.9m) pike leapt up at me. For a brief and shocking moment, we were face to face before it was sucked backwards down the pipe and off to the safety and sanctuary of the River Cherwell.

Figure 64: The author, Matt, in the second silt trap

In the days of the wooden boats, the dock was mainly used for hull scraping, caulking, repairs and painting. Caulking was the traditional process used to seal the planks, using a mixture of old shredded rope, linseed oil, tar, horsehair and horse dung. This heady cocktail was then stuffed into the gaps in the planks and painted over with pitch. This method of sealing the hull of a boat is thought to have been centuries old and used on seafaring craft, as well as barges and narrowboats. Such ancient skills have been passed down through generations of boat builders, but there are very few practitioners left in the twenty first century.

Reaching the underside of a wooden boat is awkward. In years gone by, boats would be docked down on to rockers, usually four wooden see-saws.

Figure 65: A narrowboat on the 'rockers' in the dock. Note the older roof

As the water emptied out of the dock, the boat would come to rest on these rockers, allowing it to lean to one side. Access to one side of the base of the hull was then clearly visible. By rocking boats the other way, work could be completed on the other side the craft.

Another critical job was replacing the wooden side planks of these boats. The bows and stern were particularly problematic, as the heavy planks were curved and needed to be steamed to bend them into shape. This wasn't a one-man task, so George would give Herbert a much needed and welcome hand.

One such event is remembered by Pete Downer from the 1970s. Even then, there was still the occasional need to service and repair older and traditional boats. The boiler would be filled with water and the fire lit to get ready to supply the steam. The boiler was in the belt room. This meant that the steam had to be piped over to the steamer, a large metal tube, which was situated outside the carpenter's shop. A replica steamer is still in evidence to this day and continues to be in full working order.

The old plank would then be removed from the boat and a template was made from thin wood. This template, which was used to ensure the correct shape was achieved, was then used to cut the new plank from a flat piece of oak. Nothing was wasted in the process, as the old removed plank was usually cut up and used as fuel in the boiler to steam the new one.

Once the new plank was placed in the steamer, it needed to remain inside for one hour per inch thickness of wood. Although the planks were usually two inches (5cm) thick, they would always be left for three hours, just to be certain they would be soft enough to bend. As the plank emerged from the steamer, it would be picked up with sacks to avoid the handler being burned by the heat and residual steam. This was a critical part of the process and the men would have to act fast, rushing the plank into the dock.

Inside the dock with the steamed plank in position, it was now possible to bend it to the curve of the hull by clamping it to the metal knees of the boat. If this was not done quickly enough or with insufficient skill, the plank would set at the wrong shape and would be unusable. It would then have to be discarded, doubtless resulting in recriminations and arguments all round.

The new plank would then be left overnight to harden to the correct shape. Once set, the clamps were opened and the plank was removed, cut and planed to fit tightly. When it was finally ready, it would be refitted to the boat for the last time.

Figure 66: Ian Staples rushing a newly steamed plank to his boat

Figure 67: Fitting the steamed planks on a narrowboat

Figure 68: Clamping the steamed planks on a narrowboat

Herbert was a shy man and not direct in asking for help. Pete Downer's own boatyard was situated at the old Corporation Wharf, which was off Mill Lane, below Banbury Lock and not far from Tooley's. Pete would often sense someone was watching him and he would regularly find Herbert hovering by the gate. Pete would approach to ask if he would like to come into the yard. But Herbert had come on a mission. He would explain that he needed a hand and could Pete assist him for "just a minute", but Pete knew that Herbert's 'minutes' tended to stretch somewhat.

Figure 69: Herbert Tooley standing beside the stop planks at the dock

A particular episode recalled by Pete is when he went into the dock where a boat was rocked over to one side. It was precariously held in place with old bits of wood. Pete instinctively knew what was coming. Herbert coaxed him to get under the boat, lying on his back on the muddy floor, with a large spike and a bulky and very heavy hammer.

Inside the boat, Herbert was ready, and waiting with a pre-drilled hole for the spike. Pete drove the spike through the hole Herbert had drilled, through the bottom boards and into the Keelson. He then held the spike in place with the large hammer while Herbert, inside the boat, drove a washer over the end of the spike using a hollow punch. The end of the spike was hammered over to rivet it in place. As you can tell, this is not a job for those of a nervous disposition and would certainly take more than even a 'Tooley minute'.

Even so, Pete was well used to Herbert's ruses, and gently enquired as to how many more they might have to do? Unabashed, Herbert announced "it is only another twenty four, shouldn't take too long…"

Pete was never paid for his work, it was more of a barter situation. Herbert would often give him something like a swan's neck or other boat part, in exchange for his labours. In fact, money was never Pete's motivation as he would happily toil for free. He was always pleased to help the Tooley brothers whenever he could, using the opportunity to tap into their distinctive and particular skills.

Pete wasn't the only boat builder with memories of the Tooleys. Ian Staples of Broadmoor Wooden Boats (BWB), also rented the dock on and off from 1995 to 1998. He has numerous skills when it comes to historic wooden narrowboats, and during that time, many were docked by him and repaired.

Whilst these boats are highly regarded by canal enthusiasts, their maintenance and upkeep are far from straightforward. It was during his time at Tooley's that Ian worked on well-known boats, such as *Poplar*, a 1936 butty built by Walkers of Rickmansworth, *Gort*, a 1939 motor boat built by Nursers of Braunston, *Clee*, the last boat built by Fellows, Morton & Clayton in 1947, *Clara*, a Shropshire Union Flyboat and the ironically named, *Ian*, a 1948 motor boat built by Nursers of Braunston, as well as many more. These very special craft all required specialist handling, including re-planking, shearing, plating and caulking (see overleaf).

Ian recollects that George, like his brother, was also a shy man. George always maintained his interest in the boatyard and boats. If he happened to hear that a wooden boat was in the dry dock, he'd occasionally pop down to the yard. On one memorable occasion, wooden motorboat *Gort* was in the dock being worked upon. Ian invited George in for a cup of tea to have a look at the boat, and realised that George was taking a keen interest in his

Figure 70: NB Ian under planking repair in the dock

Figure 71: The painted side panel of NB Gort

handiwork. After a close inspection, George leaned back and declared, "it was all right". This was quite a compliment from the man himself.

Figure 72: George Tooley inspecting Ian's work

They continued their conversation which turned to the job of fixing the rampers. The rampers are spikes which are driven vertically down through pre-drilled holes in the side planks into the plank below. These are spaced between the knees and are fitted to stop the planks from flexing independently and to tie them together. George told Ian to make sure that these are fitted on the inside of the boat to stop ingress of water. Ian was pleased by George's interest and observations. He was very happy that an expert on wooden boats had looked over his work and commented on it. George was a man of few words and by saying "it was all right" was almost a seal of approval.

There are far fewer wooden boats around these days, but Tooley's Boatyard still has the facilities and skills needed to keep them afloat. However, some of the techniques and methods of working aren't always fully understood by those outside of the waterways community. This can occasionally give rise to awkward situations.

Some tasks can be particularly dirty and smelly, such as caulking a wooden boat and then painting it with a tar coating known as calico, often commonly referred to as 'charlie'. It was during one of these jobs when a man strode confidently into the yard shop and asked for me. He stated that he was from the Environmental Health and that there were complaints about the smell. An accusation had been made that we were burning petrol on the site. I was most put out, saying that we would not be so irresponsible, that the works conducted were repairing a wooden boat using techniques that go back over two hundred years. "In fact," I explained, "the smell comes from boiling up tar, pitch and horse manure." The official went silent, looked down at his clipboard and failing to find the 'tar, pitch and horse manure' section of tick boxes, promptly left. I have always been concerned about running a noisy and smelly works next to a shopping centre but I'm assuming he must have been on our side, as we heard no more about it. After all, we were here first.

Figure 73: Household copper used as a boiler to make 'charlie'

The Arrival of the Diesel Engine

In 1912, the Bolinder diesel engine was introduced to power narrowboats. This revolutionised the carrying of cargo. Once again, the boatyard developed new skills to service and maintain these new types of boat engines.

Figure 74: Pete Downer's Bolinder engine

It was the arrival of the diesel engine in the 1920s, which probably led to the next development in the yard. At the north end of the dock there are four brick columns which were designated to hold a new fixed roof. It was designed to allow the stern of the boat to be placed under cover, as the majority of the work was done at the rear of the boats in the dock. It would allow engines and working parts to be protected from the elements. In addition, there was an old wooden frame covering part of the dock; it was originally on rails allowing it to be moved up and down the length of the chamber to cover anyone working at any particular part of a boat.

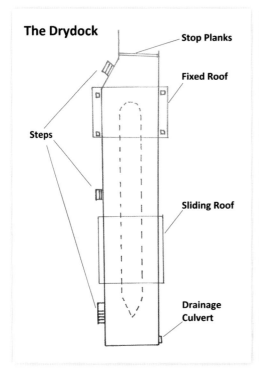

Figure 75: Plan of the dry dock in the 1920s

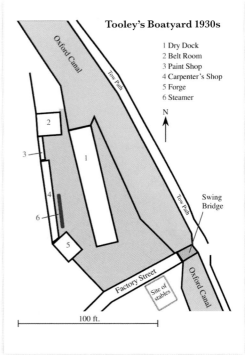

Figure 76: A map of Tooley's Boatyard in the 1930s

This frame can still be seen in place underneath the new, modern, watertight roof. It is testimony to its longevity and robust construction that it has survived, largely intact. Made from old, reclaimed boat timbers, close inspection reveals nail holes in the side planks and that the larger uprights had formed part of the keelson, which ran the length of the hull of a boat. Notches can also be seen showing the inside which would have allowed water in the bilge to move easily.

Figure 77: Rob Pointon painting in the dock

Figure 78: Ian Staples narrowboat, Bedworth, in the dock

This 'make do and mend' roof was constructed over a period of around thirty years. It was started in the 1960s by adding wood to the timber frame. It was gradually extended to run the full length of the dock and was eventually finished by the end of the 1980s.

Figure 79: The dry dock before the roof was completed

The dock continues to thrive, with around one hundred boats being worked on every year. Most boats are modern, requiring the usual jobs such as hull blacking and routine servicing, but occasionally something more challenging will arise, requiring the use of older, more unique skills, maybe even needing a bespoke part to be made in the incomparable Tooley's forge.

The Forge

Figure 80: The author, Matt, in the forge

The craft of working iron goes back thousands of years. It is such an important time in our history that it even has an era of time named after it! It was introduced to Britain at the start of the said, Iron Age, around 700BC. The skills needed to produce quality ironwork remain the same today, the key difference being the types of materials and fuel used. The blacksmith was a significant member of the boatyard, especially when boats were horse drawn, as horses regularly needed to be shod. Essential, often bespoke metal parts were also needed for boats, including nails, rivets and spikes. Such work alone was insufficient to sustain the business. Therefore, when work on the boats became slack, the forge would be used by local trade people to shoe their horses, fit metal rims to cartwheels or provide other vital metal work services for the town.

Figure 81: The forge in the 1980s

These types of yard were common in the 1700s and they were often referred to as 'jobber' yards. Small businesses would come together to provide a service; in this case carpenters and blacksmiths worked together to build and repair boats.

The forge at Tooleys is believed to have been built around the same time as the dock yard in 1778 and has changed very little over the years. It is now a scheduled Ancient Monument. A free-standing red brick structure, it is topped off with a red tile roof. The brick work is a single-phase Flemish bond, but the eaves are detailed. Close inspection reveals the irregular handmade bricks of that time.

Figure 82: The forge 2018

89

Figure 83: Inside the forge

Inside, the floor is fashioned from uneven bricks and paved stone. Upon this sits a thick wooden bench made from the reclaimed elm timber of a former working boat. There are now glazed windows and electric lights, but traditionally it would have been considerably darker inside. This suited the blacksmith, who could gauge the temperature of the metal by its subtle change in colour, as it heated up or cooled down.

The metal the blacksmith used was wrought iron, as it had a high carbon content, which made it very malleable. The wrought iron was supplied in large blocks of metal called a 'bloom'. This would then be shaped into stock sizes, which prepared it for further specific uses. Teams of blacksmiths, known as 'strikers', would offer their services to various forges. Modern smithies now use mild steel, as it is stronger and comes ready made in all shapes and stock sizes.

Originally, charcoal was used to fuel the fire, but this has now been replaced by forging coke. This burns at a higher temperature and is less toxic. It also has smaller lumps which allows the metal to be put into the heat of the fire without disrupting it.

The hearth's ancient roots are all too obvious with the chimney needing additional support to prevent it collapsing. To one side, there is an electric motor, which was installed in 1948. This forces air into the fire and creates temperatures hot enough to melt metal. The air blast would have originally been provided by a set of bellows, most probably the weighted double action kind made from iron, ash and leather. This was a manual job, usually done by a lad as young as ten or eleven. They soon learned the general rule of thumb, that more air means more heat. At the side of the hearth is a water tank and this is called the bosh. This provides the water to cool the tuyere; this is a water jacket which protects the pipe taking the air from the bellows to be directed into the middle of the fire. Without this cover the tuyere would burn out, as it is subjected to temperatures in excess of 1300 degrees centigrade.

Steel Heat/Colour Chart

Colour	C	F
Faint Red	600	1112
Dark Red	700	1292
Cherry Red	800	1472
Dull Orange	900	1652
Orange	950	1742
Lemon Yellow	1000	1832
Yellow	1050	1922
Bright Yellow	1100	2012
White	1200	2192
Glowing White	1300	2372

Figure 86: Forging temperatures chart

Figure 85: Working in the forge

The size of the fire in this forge is quite compact, making it ideally suited for the manufacture of horseshoes. In general, two sets would be made; one to go on the horse at once and the other would become a spare set. Legend has it that if a horse refused to cooperate, its legs would be tied together and it would be turned upside down to allow it to be shod, something we simply couldn't imagine today.

An extract from Sheila Stewart's fictional book, Ramlin Rose, based on interviews with real boaters expertly sets the scene,

'Dad were goin to warn Mr Plester, the Banbury blacksmith, to get Charley's shoes ready. Mr Plester had his smithy 'gen Tooley's yard. There'd been a smith there since the Cut were first cut, and many of 'em was Plesters. Folk had only to say, 'Boatee Ramlin's Charley needs shoddin' and Mr Plester would know zackly how much iron was needed. 'Once shod, never forgot', yet he shod oondreds of 'orses, bewry 'orses, coal 'orse. Boat 'orses in them days.'

There are many anecdotes, mostly unwritten, about the 'Plesters' family and their association with the forge. Perhaps the best known and most often told, is that of the blacksmith's wife, Mrs Plester, who was one of the few people to be able to read. Boaters would bring her a letter and she would read it to them. They would then give their response and she would write it for them. The forge was full of letters; some waiting for her to read, and others the responses she had written, which were to be collected by the boaters.

There is an arch underneath the hearth; this was most probably a charcoal or coke store. The bulk of the fuel would have been kept outside, but it would have been brought inside in batches to keep it dry, to stop it from spitting when it is added to the fire.

Turning to the people who worked in the forge, we are able to discern a great deal about what they were like from the clues they've left behind. It is highly probable that the last blacksmith to have worked this forge was right handed and about five feet ten inches tall. This is because the anvil is set up for a right-handed person as the bick (the pointed bit also known as a beak) is on the left.

Figure 87: The anvil in the forge

We can be confident about the last blacksmith's height because the anvil would have been set at the correct level for his stature. This would be high enough for him (female blacksmiths were very rare!) to clench his fist and for his knuckles to brush the face of the anvil. This would serve two purposes, the first being that the hammer would naturally fall flat so as to not leave marks in the metal; the second is that if the height was wrong then the blacksmith would have to strain to hold the hammer at an uncomfortable and awkward angle in an effort to prevent marking the metal.

As for the lad who had the job of working the bellows, he would have been apprenticed to the smith. His parents would have paid money for their son to be taken on as a trainee. The apprenticeship would have lasted anywhere between four to eight years. After that time at the smith's discretion, the apprentice would have been allowed to leave, but only on the smith's say so. Obtaining such permission would often prove difficult as the blacksmith would not be keen for his protégé to leave. After all, he would lose an experienced and skilled hand and the former apprentice could even set up in competition against him. If the blacksmith died, then the right to keep and work the apprentice was passed onto the smith's widow. This was an important consideration because the widow of the smith would no longer have any form of income. She would therefore need to keep the apprentice as the breadwinner.

I was lucky enough to meet Jack Plester's son, John. He was the last apprentice blacksmith in the forge and he told me about the day that he gave up blacksmithing. He was working in the forge, with his dad, making a hitching pin for a waggon. They were making this pin out of a 4ins cube of metal, which must have been unbearably hot. They had to forge this cube into the correct shape. Jack would heat up the piece of metal to the correct temperature, then John's job was to hit it with a sledge hammer. After four hours of working with the heat, and shattered from the back-breaking job of repeatedly striking the metal with the heavy sledge, John had had enough and realised that blacksmithing was not for him.

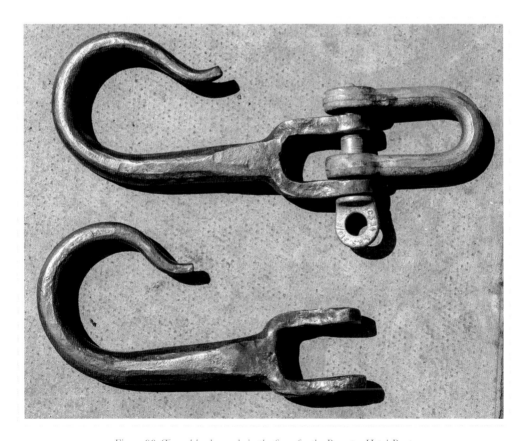

Figure 88: Tunnel hooks made in the forge for the Bywater Hotel Boats

Although apprenticeships are no longer served in Tooleys forge, there is still the opportunity to learn some of the blacksmiths' traditional skills during special forging days held at the yard. Metal work of varying kinds are still completed for the modern boats requiring specialist attention during their time in the dock. These are covered in more detail in chapter four. In 2014, a metal arbour was made in the forge by master blacksmith, Clive Sanderson. This was a centre piece to a display at the Chelsea Flower Show, which won a silver award.

Figure 90: The arbour being assembled before going to the Chelsea Flower Show

Figure 91: The arbour at the Chelsea Flower Show

Carpenter's Shop

Figure 92: Inside the carpenter's shop

To deal with the diversity of jobs that are needed on boats, the yard was extended to accommodate a combined carpentry shop, chandlery and paint shop. The carpenter's store is a lean-to structure partially walled with salvaged boat timbers. It was very makeshift and cobbled together from bits and pieces. Most of these were from demolition sites using all manner of discarded material. This building was renovated during the 1990s redevelopment.

Figure 93: The carpenter's shop in the 1980s

Figure 94: The carpenter's shop, showing planks recycled from wooden boats

The front of the building is made from elm boards which had been at the bottom of boats, where evidence of mud worm can clearly be seen on them. In addition, the workbench and shelves were also made from reclaimed boat timbers.

Figure 95: Evidence of mudworm on the re-used boards in the carpenter's shop

Various tools and clamps were kept in here, but the main work of repairing boats was done in the dock. Large timbers were laid across the southern end of the dock and the dock itself was used as a saw pit.

Herbert Tooley famously used his trusty adze, a mattock type tool, for shaping wood during the boat building process. He was known to say that his adze was so old that it had been used to build the Ark! Although it was strongly suspected that it had had at least two new heads and three new handles, Herbert insisted that it was his one and only. And whilst it is debatable as to whether Herbert's adze was actually used on the Ark, there is little doubt that many of the techniques he used in wooden boat building date back thousands of years.

Figure 96: Herbert Tooley with his adze in the dry dock

Paint Shop

Working narrowboats were traditionally painted in the corporate colours of the company who owned them, principally to make their identification easier and more distinctive. In the early days, boats were painted with their name, the name of the company who owned them and a registration number. The lettering was basic and functional.

Later working boats were decorated more elaborately, with the canal folk art of 'roses and castles', which was widely in use over a hundred years ago. Landscape scenes, which included fairy tale castles, were painted directly on to the cabin sides, inside and out. The origin of the roses and castles style is difficult to define and a topic of much debate. Some people cited a possible connection with Romany gypsies and their passion for painting their wagons. This connection may, understandably, have been made due to the itinerant nature of life for gypsies and boaters alike. The two groups were, however, quite separate and distinct in many ways. Many of the families who became boaters over generations, were descendants from the original navvies and labourers that had worked building the cut in each local area.

Others, claimed that boaters painted their boats prior to its introduction by the gypsies to their caravans. It has also been suggested that women arriving into the boating life, led to the trend of decorating and personalising boats. There is little evidence to strongly substantiate any one of these theories. Whatever the origins, for many of the boaters this picturesque romanticism allowed them to depict the ideal homestead on the side of their boat, reinforcing the adage that 'an Englishman's home is his castle'.

Roses and castles and other British flowers were also painted on water cans, stools, lamps, door panels, horses' harnesses and much more. These additional adornments were added to the boat where the painter or boater thought necessary and when money allowed. This styling was common all over the canal system, although it was the Oxford and Grand Union canals which had the greatest number of boats painted in this fashion.

Figure 98: The last Buckby water can painted by Herbert Tooley

Every working boatyard would ordinarily have a resident painter, or would at least be able to employ one locally. Having such skill was highly prized and a great deal of prestige was bestowed on individual painters. Moreover, most would have their own unique style or 'signature'. To paraphrase Shakespeare's assertion that, 'a rose is a rose by any other name', may not be applicable in the case of the traditional boat rose painters. Nigel Crowe, in his 1994 book, Canals remarks,

'Herbert Tooley's roses have been called 'succulent and famous' differing in style from those of Harry Taylor, Frank Nurser, Harry Atkins and many others instantly recognisable to the expert boat signage historian.'

The origins of the Tooley approach is explored in this extract from Tony Lewery's sumptuous encyclopedia of canal art, Flowers Afloat. Here, he comments on the roots of the Tooley oeuvre,

'The style of the paintwork now associated with the Tooleys may once more owe its ancestry to the Nursers. Ernest Carvell was a boat builder from Braunston who was employed by old George to work at Banbury in the early days partly because, according to Herbert, he was adept at painting roses and castles. … George Tooley senior did most of the decoration necessary, having learned to do it himself by watching Carvell at work. He (George) was clearly a very naturally gifted all-round craftsman…'

He comes to the following conclusion about George junior and Herbert,

'Both brothers were primarily boat builders, spending most of their time working with heavy oak and elm planks and iron knees, which made the delicacy and gentleness of their painted work all the more remarkable.'

As previously mentioned, Tom Rolt was particularly fascinated with this aspect of the yard's work. One of very few people to be able to record seeing all three Tooleys demonstrate their individual skills, he was determined to make good use of their specialist talents on his own boat, *Cressy*.

Evidence of their painting survives to this day in the Paint Shop. This workspace is more of a store full of old tins of paint, mostly dating from the 1950s; it's all the good stuff, full of lead and much else that would doubtless cause apoplexy to any self-respecting health and safety inspector.

The Paint Shop has a rather well-known door; it was made from the planks of the back cabin of a boat. According to Herbert Tooley, around 1928, the horse-drawn boat *Fair Trader* was converted into a motor boat and was one of the first working boats to undergo such a modification. It was this boat, which supplied the wood used to make the front door. Closer inspection allows an intriguing insight into the past workings of these highly skilled artisans. On opening the door, it is still possible to see a layer of paint of around two inches deep which built up over many years. This is the very door each of the Tooleys used to clean their paint brushes at the end of a job.

By contrast, modern leisure boats tend to be painted to individual customer's needs and tastes. Traditional skills and styles are still employed during this process; boats are stripped back to bare metal and painted with six to eight coats of paint. Completion takes six to seven weeks and they are finished off by sign writing the name of the boat and any other information as required. Sometimes, the long-established practice of adorning roses and castles is utilised, or other similar, elaborate artwork as requested by the owner. Whilst it may not match the work of the Tooleys, the spirit and essence of the past lives on through the skill of today's modern artists.

Figure 99: The paint shop door showing layers of paint. The wood is from NB Fair Trader

100: Jamie Simmons making the 15th anniversary gates in 2017

101: Jez Barrington painting in the dock

Belt Room

Figure 102: Belt shop machinery

The belt room building dates from the 1930s. It was another of those 'add-on' rooms which sprang up out of necessity. Housing the plethora of belt driven machinery required in an expanding boatyard, it wheedled its way into the yard finding its own space amongst the hotch-potch of buildings and equipment. It is a wooden structure which is bolted to the floor. Originally, it had an 'apex' roof, but after the 1990s restorations and rebuild, this was lost in order to accommodate it underneath the museum bridge. It was in a poor state and needed a good deal of attention before it could be reinstated to the yard in a safe condition.

This type of machinery, especially in good running order, has become rare. There are some local examples at Hook Norton Brewery, near Banbury, and also at Coombe Mill, near Witney in Oxfordshire. These are kept in working order by hours of dedicated loving care and attention by skilled enthusiasts. I remember from my archaeological days going to assess derelict buildings which were earmarked for demolition, only to find the machinery gone by the time we got there. I am very pleased to see this apparatus still operating, as it continues to be of great interest to the public.

It had always been intended to show the belt room in all its original glory, with the machines performing their many tasks in the same way they had done during the 1930s and '40s. The Health and Safety executive had other ideas however, pointing out that such a display was inherently dangerous. In truth, belt rooms had always been places of considerable danger throughout former industrial times. Moving around in this unprotected space was fraught with danger; a trip or fall into the path of a fast-moving belt would often result in fatalities or serious, life changing injury. The belts themselves could be unreliable too, often snapping and flying off in all directions. There are very few remaining, fully working belt rooms left in the United Kingdom, so it was a huge disappointment to think that this wonderful spectacle would be lost to modern generations.

The Health and Safety Executive was therefore asked to help solve this particularly challenging problem. Whilst the reality was that it should have been closed down by the Health and Safety at Work Act 1974, the hope was that a pragmatic solution could be found. Perseverance paid off,

Figures 103: The milling machine in the belt shop

Figures 104: Big marine engine in belt room

Figures 10.5: Big twin pot engine in belt room

and it was agreed that demonstrations could take place provided the machinery was slowed down to approximately 1/10th of its normal running speed, and rigorous risk assessments completed.

Despite their renowned frugality and ability to make do and mend, it is interesting to note that the largest capital investment the Tooleys made for the yard was the purchase of a Lister engine to drive the belts. It cost £46 in 1943 and gives an indication of essential work they were undertaking throughout the war years. The importance of this belt room cannot be overstated; if a boat owner requires parts today, it's a simple matter of ordering online or by phone for next-day delivery. For most of the twentieth century no such service was available meaning that everything they needed had to be made from scratch. This is what the belt room workshop was all about. These metal and woodworking lathes allowed the Tooleys to cut, shape, tool and craft just about anything a boater might need.

During the 1930s the belt room was powered by steam. Herbert told Pete Downer that this power source was a second-hand engine from a Mann Steam Lorry. As with all things 'steam', it required a good deal of effort and maintenance to keep it running efficiently. A new solution was found in their next second-hand purchase, a Pelapone diesel engine. It was the first to be used to drive the belts and generate the electricity for the yard and house in Factory Street.

Figure 106: View from Banbury lock, towards the wharf and Factory Street

Figures 107: The boiler which made the steam for plank bending

As with all engines, it required attention from time to time. It was in use during the time of Tom Rolt's visit, but continuous use had taken its toll. Nevertheless, Rolt marvelled at their ingenuity in getting it back up and running.

108: One of the Tooley's moulds for making engine parts

This passage from Narrow Boat perfectly captures the scene,

'Most remarkable of all, when this engine broke a piston, they did not, as you would suppose, send an urgent order to the manufacturer for a spare, but set to work to make another. This meant making a wooden pattern, core and mould-box, constructing the mould in sand, melting the iron in a crucible over their small open hearth, pouring the mould and turning the casting to size. All this was done as though the task was of everyday occurrence, and the engine has run perfectly ever since.'

CHAPTER SIX

MODERN TOOLEY'S

Figure 109: The author, Matt, with Michael Portillo during filming in the dock

At the time of writing, it's important to stress that Tooley's Boatyard is very much a thriving and busy workplace. It operates in much the same way as any commercial venture and, since 2002, has undertaken various commissions on private and commercial boats alike. Although it is in very close proximity to Castle Quay shopping centre and the Banbury Museum, the boatyard receives no public subsidies, relying entirely on the success of its own ventures.

Owing in large part to its unique relationship with Tom Rolt and *Cressy*, there continues to be a fascination with the yard, attracting a great deal of media attention. Film crews, journalists and visitors from all over the world continue to frequent this jewel in Banbury's crown, enthralled by the determination of a dedicated group of people to keep traditional skills very much alive. Recent years have seen film crews from the BBC's 'Country File', and 'Great Railway Journeys' with Michael Portillo. Channel 4 and ITV have also visited, filming 'Great Canal Journeys' with Timothy West and Prunella Scales and 'Barging Round Britain' with John Sergeant. There is a clear and growing appetite to watch, interact and understand the history of this very British approach to boat building, transport, trade and leisure. Written articles and features in various newspapers and magazines have all helped to keep Tooley's legacy and current activities in the public domain.

Figure 110: A break from filming for Timothy West and Prunella Scales

A visit to the yard opens the door to a hive of activity. There's always something going on; a boat in the dock undergoing repairs, deliveries of parts, paints and new items for the chandlery, the sound of industry from within the forge, regular visitors in the café, or students arriving for their latest boating instruction course. The diverse courses on offer allow enthusiasts to learn new and distinct skills. One is blacksmithing; an intensive course during which participants produce their own forged metal work. Also on offer are formal boating qualifications which can be achieved through official Royal Yachting Association structured tuition.

On those infrequent days when there are no boats in the dock, it rarely stands idle. Enthusiastic musicians, actors, playwrights and historians flow into this ancient space with the same fervour and force as the water itself. The strange acoustics within the dock lend themselves perfectly to performance art of all kinds. Kate Saffin, a well-known canal producer, writer and actor, has performed many of her unique waterways tales here, to much acclaim.

Figure 111: Sarah Jackson hand making goods for the chandlery

Yet, the connection with music in particular, is not new to Tooley's. The telling of stories, singing of songs and playing of instruments within the canal community has always been an important part of life on the cut. Tom Rolt was well aware of the connection and marvelled at the very special link between music and the narrowboat community,

Figures 112: Alarum Theatre evening in the dock at Tooley's

113: Kate Saffin during Theatre in the Dock with Graham Currie

114: The Mikron Theatre Company performing in the dock

'Like our rural ancestors with their country songs, festivals and dances, he has to provide his own amusement, than which there is no healthier stimulant for talent. As a result many boatmen are self taught musicians, and I found that nearly every boat on the Oxford Canal carried a melodeon, a concertina or an accordion. Often of a night time I would hear the familiar strains of 'Daisy Bell' or 'Two Lovely Black Eyes' floating over the water from the cabin of a moored boat.'

Many of these traditional ballads are still played in the dock with skill and great enthusiasm, at various performances and concerts throughout the year. Instruments commonly used during the last century are regularly aired, keeping the old skills alive, providing a haunting and entertaining insight into the life of the wider boating community. These days, specialist repairs and servicing of these precious implements are hard to come by, but it wasn't always the case as Rolt observed,

'Needless to say, Herbert Tooley had become proficient in repairing these instruments, and I looked on one evening while he dexterously fitted a new key spring to a melodeon belonging to John Harwood of the 'Searchlight'. While he worked, the old boatman talked, his unhurried, rhythmical speech as soothing as a Gregorian chant. He described graphically his only journey in 'one o' they moty cars', whose speed struck him out of all reason, so great that it 'fair took the breath out of him'.'

This tradition is still alive and well within the Boatyard. Jez Barrington may not have many melodeons to work on these days, but he can often be found in his workshop repairing and fettling modern day guitars, something I'm sure the Tooleys would approve of.

In our fast-moving world of smart phones, social media, the internet, and information overload, the attraction of a slower, gentler and less complex age is perhaps understandable. It's impossible to know exactly what Herbert would make of our current 'disposable and throw-away' culture, but he would doubtless be baffled and perhaps even appalled at the needless waste. As we have seen, the Tooleys were past masters at fixing, mending and innovating, most especially at times of adversity and strain. A visit to the yard, described so perceptively by Sonia Rolt in a BBC radio interview as a 'stickleback's house' where it was 'possible to mend anything' clearly demonstrates their approach, with evidence of their ingenuity on display for all to see to this day. Wherever possible, current practices and procedures within Tooley's remain true to this traditional way of working.

As mentioned at the beginning of this chapter, there have been a number of celebrities and waterways luminaries who have taken an interest in Tooley's. Their support, encouragement and backing has been incredibly important in raising the profile of the yard and keeping it in the public eye. Special mention should be made to the actors Timothy West, whose foreword opens this book, and his wife Prunella Scales; both are widely known throughout the boating community as active campaigners for the wellbeing of canals and rivers. Although she has played a variety of highly accomplished parts throughout her career, Prunella is probably best known for her portrayal of Sybil in the legendary sitcom, Fawlty Towers. But it isn't only in the fictional Torquay Hotel that calamities and mishaps can occur. Throughout my time on the water there have been many challenges and trials. As many of us know to our cost, even the most experienced and competent boat handlers and crew can be caught out. Perhaps the biggest enemy is complacency and over-confidence.

Bill (Boswell) told me that his granddad always said, that on the water you learn a new thing every day. In fact, just sitting down and chatting with other boaters it is possible to learn something different, as there are a myriad of ways to do things on board. He contended that, 'You're not a proper boatman until you have fallen in the water.' The first time I understood what he meant was on our restaurant boat – *Rosamund the Fair*. I was well used to walking about the boat – especially when we were on it sixteen hours a day – I thought nothing of walking down the gunnels with a box of wine on each shoulder while the boat was moving. Simple.

It was a warm summer's day, when I was about to skipper the 72ft (22m) passenger vessel for a Sunday lunch cruise, which was tied up at the Trout Inn at Wolvercote. I jumped on the gunnel at the bow and confidently made my way down the narrow lip towards the stern, something I had done hundreds of times before. This time I snagged my foot on a fender line and slipped. My hand instinctively dropped to the hand rail on the boat for safety. Unfortunately, I already had a firm grip on an orange, so my hand bounced off and I instantly knew I was going in. I hit my knee on the way down, splashing loudly as I hit the water. I found myself sitting on the bottom of the sloping river bed with my head just out of a very cold undercurrent. It was then that I realised everyone in the busy pub garden had rushed to the bank to stare at me.

As I strained to regain my dignity, I couldn't imagine things becoming any worse. Nevertheless, I heard a fuss building about six feet above me and I witnessed the landlady of the Trout, who was rather partial to her gin, barging her way through the crowd to see what was going on. In her rapid drive through the crowd towards the edge, she lost her footing and fell in. She landed beside me, up to her neck in water. She stared blankly at me, clearly in shock. Then in a desperate attempt to save face she began shouting, 'I have jumped in to save you.' Well, if you are going to fall in for the first time, you might as well make it a good one. As you might imagine, I was far more cautious after that!

Falling in is nothing compared to the terrors of fixing toilets on boats. It's a strange phenomenon, but all boaters throughout the world have at least one, usually more, tales of woe regarding their lavatory. As a boat fitter and builder, it's an area I try to avoid wherever possible, but sometimes there's just nowhere to hide.

On one occasion, a passing boater dropped in to the boatyard complaining about a blocked loo. My heart always sinks when these tasks surface. No matter how loyal you are to friends and long held customers, there's a propensity for things to be tricky and technically challenging. In this case, the toilet cubicle was very small, only about 3 feet square. To access the actual pan, I had to go in and close the door behind me. I knelt down in front of it and discovered it was the type that made me especially nervous, it was a macerator, meaning that it chews everything up and pumps in into a holding tank. I could see that it was blocked and probably under a lot of pressure…

Like an explosive expert defusing a bomb, I very gingerly started to gently feel the pipe from the macerator to the holding tank. I was just considering my options to solve this difficulty when the inevitable happened! A Jubilee clip holding the pressurised pipe gave way and in a moment of horror it completely dowsed me in minced up human waste. I turn around to find, in cartoon style, my outline projected on the wall behind me. I'm sure you'll believe me when I tell you that I have never made this mistake twice!

There are times when dealing with the proposed changes at the yard that I am reminded of the above anecdote. Feeling my way around the countless obstacles to securing and safeguarding this precious place is reminiscent of checking the jubilee clip. I'm never quite sure if it's on tight enough or whether it's all about to blow…

What the future holds for the yard is far from clear. Nevertheless, there is little doubt that this jumble of old buildings, squeezed as they are, beneath the huge shopping centre, continues to command both affection and respect from a loyal, steadfast and growing group of supporters and enthusiasts. There are of course, conflicting ideas as to how Tooley's should be run and represented within an ever-changing environment; for some it should be 'preserved' and exhibited under controlled conditions, opening only on special occasions as a 'visitor attraction'. On the other hand, there are those who strongly believe that it should remain a vibrant and lively work space with the boating community at its heart. So, what does the future look like?

The Future of Tooley's

Figure 115: NB Venice in the dock

It's fair to say that Banbury's relationship with the canal has often been fraught, and at times, even hostile. In the late 1970s the author and authority on all matters concerning waterways, Hugh McKnight, dedicated a section of his tome, 'The Shell Book of Inland Waterways' to Banbury and its future. His observations are remarkably prophetic,

'You cannot help liking the place, even if the actions of local philistines at various stages in its history have left a number of scars... Our own times are in some ways little different. Nondescript plate-glass shop fronts have replaced centuries old properties, and the major part of the market square frontages are currently threatened by redevelopment (promises have been made to build mock replicas of the best elevations!). Worst action of all was the conversion in the early 1960s of a well-designed and spacious canal basin by the lock, right in the centre of town, into a hideous waste of tarmac and wire netting – the Banbury bus station.

The post-war period between the decline of commercial traffic and the growth
of pleasure boating has much to answer for! While Banbury may not boast
a location with the potential of the waterfront at, say, York or Richmond-on-
Thames, its utter disregard for the Oxford Canal is alarming. If the situation
changes with the passing of years, these words will at least serve as a reminder that
the townsfolk of Banbury were slow to appreciate one of their greatest latent assets.

To its credit, Banbury has the largest cattle market in Europe, some excellent
shops (including the best ironmongers and seed merchants), and Banbury cakes,
which are still made to a 300-year-old recipe. Herbert Tooley's renowned
narrow-boat dock somehow survives in its traditional faded form, clinging to
a patch of land above the lock. Neither the bus station, nor a new road bridge
and embankment could dislodge Mr Tooley. Patronise him if you can.'

Figure 116: The swing bridge at Tooley's in the 1970s

Certainly, Banbury has changed a good deal since the 1970s. It's seen a huge rise in the population, almost doubling, over this period. (Census 1971 – 26,540 to 2011 – 46,853) Sadly, we've lost the cattle market referred to above as well as the ironmongers and seed merchants and of course, Herbert Tooley. But at least Banbury cakes are still around.

The 1990s provided a huge opportunity for Banbury to heed McKnight's portents and embrace the centuries old canal as the living heart of the town. The Castle Quay development in the town centre was to be built right on its banks, providing the chance to incorporate the waterway into the heart of the building. Many towns and cities had long been aware of the commercial advantages of facing and embracing their waterways into urban development, most noticeably perhaps, Birmingham where the renaissance of canals is universally regarded as highly successful. As you can see in the photographs from that time, Banbury's chance to emulate the success of similar towns and cities was missed when the developers turned the architecture and buildings away from the canal, effectively endorsing McKnight's observation that Banbury has been slow to appreciate one of its greatest assets.

Figure 117: Castle Quay development in the 1990s

Figure 118: Castle Quay and Tooley's abandoned in the 1990s

It would be quite wrong however, to conclude that the people of Banbury don't appreciate the canal; the sheer numbers of visitors, every October to the Canal Day festival is testimony to their continued interest and support for this ribbon of water. Moreover, the latest (2018) proposals for new developments within the town centre appear to be sympathetic to waterside life. A number of propositions for cafes, a cinema, hotel and shops all facing the canal have received approval and open enthusiasm from the people of the town. Most importantly, the significance of Tooley's within these planned changes has been recognised.

Figure 119: Banbury Canal Day

Figure 120: Di Downer spinning during Banbury Canal Day

Figure 121: Canal artist Bruce Coleman decorating a jug

Figure 122: Philip Tree, an RYA instructor, wearing traditional costume in the dock

The devil is always in the detail it seems, but if the suggestions for the safeguarding and preservation of this unique historical yard within the next phase of Banbury's growth are upheld and financed, then the future may be secure. In fairness, most people other than the boating community are largely unaware of the history and deep heritage of the canals and even less so, yards like Tooley's. Yet it's a source of considerable delight to see and hear the reaction of first-time visitors to Tooley's when they discover the wonders on offer. Many become 'friends' of the yard and all things connected, evangelising to everyone they meet about the importance of maintaining this unique and quirky working boatyard. Such enthusiasm is always welcome, but Tooley's has entered a new and challenging chapter where support through finance is urgently needed. It is staggering to think that it has survived as a commercial and self-funding concern (often only just) throughout its long history. There appears to be an increasing groundswell of opinion supporting the notion that something this precious, falls firmly into the public heritage funding arena.

Historic Narrowboat Hardy

Figure 123: Hardy breasted up with NB Gertrude

Perhaps the best way to illustrate the importance of Tooley's is to show what can be achieved. Throughout this book it will have become clear that there are many of us who are passionate about the past, present and future of the waterways. On a personal note, one of the most difficult things to witness and accept is the unnecessary destruction of salvageable heritage boats. These hand-built wooden craft are becoming a very rare sight on our canals and rivers.

When I recently heard about one such boat, I decided it was time to act. It's easy to lament lost heritage, yet far more difficult to actually do something tangible about it. So it was that on a damp May morning, I set off to Puddlebanks, near Braunston, on the Oxford Canal, to have a look at the very sorry remains of a once proud cargo carrier. Built in 1940 by Nursers, it was intended to shift cargo for the war effort.

These photographs (shown opposite) from an excellent article written for
Narrow Boat magazine in 2013 by David Blagrove shows Hardy hard at work.
As you can see this craft was still carrying coal to Banbury as late as the 1960s.

Figure 124: Hardy moored opposite Tooley's Boatyard

Figure 125: Hardy moored at Banbury coal wharf

Figure 126: Hardy entering Banbury lock

Figure 127: Hardy on the Oxford Canal

As we approached, we were met with the stark reality of a sunken wooden narrowboat. But there was something about Hardy that was different, something real, visceral and vital. This was a boat that wanted to be saved and to have a life again.

The process of re-floating a half-submerged wooden boat is far from easy, but we'd come prepared. We had an assortment of gear ranging from a pump, buckets, tin plate, nails and all sorts of paraphernalia including a nice, fresh, smelly bucket of charlie, looked after by Jamie Simmons, one of the skilled crew from Tooley's.

We set about the task with the care and urgency of a team of paramedics determined to save a patient. The boat had been inundated for four years. It was sitting on the canal bed full of water and all kinds of rubbish and debris. We set up the pump on the exposed roof and started to force the filthy water out. We soon realised that the pump was having little or no effect as the water was coming in faster than the pump could handle. Thankfully, we had an experienced hand along with us to help and guide on the lifting process. Ian Staples has a long history of working with all kinds of narrowboats, including many restorations. It soon became obvious, that if we were to float this boat, we'd have to plug all of the holes in the hull, even as we continued to pump the water out.

In the end, we were forced to get into the hull and bail out the fetid water manually, gradually reducing the level by a mere six inches. As we bailed, more holes were revealed, and we swiftly filled them with oakum. After four hours of repeating this operation, Hardy finally began to lift from the canal bed. The joy of seeing this proud old narrowboat afloat, was tempered by the reality of its condition. It looked like a complete wreck. It was damp and musty with six inches of thick canal silt on the floor. Water still trickled through the few gaps we'd missed on the sides. Several aquatic friends had made this place their home, but it was now time for the crayfish, frogs and wildly flapping assortment of fish to leave. Other discarded, familiar boating items, sodden reminders of the last occupants lay abandoned in the bowels of the boat. There was an eerie feeling that their presence had somehow been trapped within this hand-crafted wooden structure.

Of course, the oakum filler was only a temporary measure and wouldn't guarantee a safe passage back to Banbury. More substantial measures were needed to cover the fist size holes peppered throughout the hull. Just when I thought we were good to go, I heard Jamie calmly call for a hand as both of his were stuffed into a newly emerged leak in the hold. Looking like the little boy with his finger in the dyke, I just hoped he could hold out for a few moments longer. We cut and fitted metal plates, adding a layer of charlie over the temporary oakum fillings and nailed them in place to seal them off. Using all of our collective skills, and after many hours of determined effort, the team had Hardy ready to be towed back to Banbury, a couple of weeks later.

When we returned to bring the boat back to Banbury, some of our crew, Sarah Jackson and Jamie Simmons, had already brought Tooley's own narrowboat, the *Dancing Duck* up to Puddlebanks over the two previous days. Thankfully, the *Duck's* engine had been designed to cope with towing and was eager to show off some pulling power. With the help of Graham Symons we fitted a 'swan's neck' to Hardy, to help us steer and began to think about the journey home.

Figure 128: Towing back NB Hardy to Tooley's Boatyard in 2018

This was a voyage full of challenges. During our two and a half days heading back to Banbury, we encountered a few interesting tests and trials. We got stuck in a lock on the Napton Flight, the narrowest on the Oxford Canal, but after fitting chains and pulling the spreading sides back in, Hardy thankfully went through. On the second day, we were grateful for the help of volunteers, Steve Robinson and Chris Baldwin. On approaching Broadmoor Lock we got stuck fast on the unseen, submerged wall of the canal, which had eroded away. It was just the right depth to jam the wooden narrowboat solid. Eventually, we managed to prise Hardy off but not without incident. I was stranded on a floating tree stump on the far side of the canal, and Jamie perched precariously on the gunnel side of the boat. How he avoided a ducking in the canal, I will never know; fortunately for him, Sarah and Ian were close at hand and just managed to grab hold of him!

Figure 129: Jamie Simmons being rescued by Sarah Jackson, Ian Staples and Steve Robinson on NB Hardy

Now the boat is moored outside Tooley's and with the help of dedicated volunteers, the hold has been cleaned up and refreshed. We have discovered other areas requiring urgent attention and begun the much-needed repair process. Cosmetically, there's a great deal to do before it's returned to anything like the glory days, but at Tooley's we relish the challenge. Once inside the dry dock, we can carry out a full examination and assessment and begin the process of restoration.

Figure 130: Ian Staples caulking NB Hardy in Tooley's dry dock

Figure 131: Hardy in the dry dock at Tooley's

In conclusion, I have a personal vision for the future of Tooley's. I firmly believe that a structured approach to developing traditional boat building and maintenance skills could be at the heart of this yard. It could become the centre of excellence for apprenticeships in this field, specialising in creating and constructing wooden narrowboats using proven and tested methods. Moreover, just as the Tooleys themselves progressed and adapted through eras of horse drawn, steam and finally diesel powered narrowboats, we could easily meet the 21st century challenge of the eco-friendly battery and hybrid period ahead. It would be a very natural and wholly appropriate way of securing the future working progression of the yard.

The alternative is to preserve it in aspic until it begins to fade to the point of irrelevance, where perhaps suggestions such as those that surfaced during the 1990s once again come to the fore. During the development of the Castle Quay shopping centre, the initial proposals were that the dry dock should be turned into a memorial flower bed and the forge a food dispensing kiosk. It's hard to imagine such an ignominious end for Tooley's and even harder still to think it was even considered. Such ideas and proposals were exactly what Tom Rolt came up against after World War II. His determination, as we have seen, prevented the wholesale destruction and filling in of vast tracts of waterways across the country, waterways that would have been lost forever. Such a fate for Tooley's is frankly unthinkable and unnecessary. Rolt had a particular passion for artisans and their skills. He would often be found immersed in the sounds and smells of the boatyard. In particular, he loved the 'wheelwright shop' which is better known to us as the carpenter's shop. Perhaps the final words should be those of Sonia Rolt, when in the BBC radio interview referred to earlier, she summed up Tom Rolt's views about lost skills and cultures,

'He knew and loved the wheelwright shop, he could not be so interested in the museum of the wheelwright shop.'

BIBLIOGRAPHY

The Shell Book of Inland Waterways –
Hugh McKnight - 1982 (Book Club
Associates London)

The Oxford Canal – Hugh J Compton
- 1976 (David & Charles Publishers Ltd)

English Canals Explained –
Stan Yorke 2008 (Countryside Books)

Nicholson Waterways Guide
No 1 Grand Union, Oxford & South East
2006 (Harper Collins Publishers Ltd)

Canals – Nigel Crowe - English Heritage
- 1994 (B T Batsford Ltd)

Narrow Boat – L T C Rolt 1948
(Eyre & Spottiswoode)

A History of Banbury –
William Potts - (Gulliver Press)
1978 Edition

Britain's Canal and River Craft –
E Paget-Tomlinson (Moorland
Publishing) 1979

Canal Barges & Narrow Boats –
Peter L Smith (Shire Publications Ltd)
No. 8 1975

A Pictorial History of Canal Craft –
Peter L Smith (B T Batsford Ltd) 1979

Green & Silver –
L T C Rolt (The IWA Ireland) 1993

Building Britain's Canals –
David Gladwin (K A F Brewin Books) 1988

Narrowboats Explained –
Trevor Yorke (Countryside Books) 2009

The University of Birmingham –
Archaeological Recording at Tooley's
Boatyard. (Aug 2000)

[Their references – Hartland G J C (1969)
'The Boatbuilding Yard at Banbury' Cake
and Cockhorse 4.4 55-57. Clarke, m (1982)
'The Origins of the Narrowboat',
Canal & Riverboat 55-60.

Flowers Afloat – Tony Lewery
(David & Charles) 1996

Our Canal in Oxford – Mark Davies
and Catherine Robinson (1999)

Britain's Canals, a National treasure
in 100 must see objects. 2012 Pub:
Coolcanals. Martine O'Callaghan
& Philippa Greenwood.

The Boy Off the Boats –
Joyce Beasley (2018)
(unpublished manuscript)

THANKS TO

Special thanks are due to Anette Fuhrmeister of The History Press for permission to use quotes from Tom Rolt's Narrow Boat.

The Banbury Guardian have also been extremely helpful during the research of this book. Waterways World have been invaluable as a source of information, particularly Herbert Tooley's interview with them in 1982. Their assistance with the 'Hardy' article is also greatly appreciated. The credit for the 1960s photos of Hardy is to David Martin.

I am indebted to the Canal and River Trust Heritage Department for permission to use images from their Waterways Archive. Particular thanks go to John Benson and Phil Emery for their interest and assistance. The permissions department at the British Library have also been very helpful.

ILLUSTRATION ACKNOWLEDGEMENTS

Photographs and drawings are reproduced with the kind permission of the following individuals and organisations:

Rosie Burke: 21, 27, 28, 32, 46, 67, 68, 76, 114, 121

Pete Downer: 3, 43, 53, 98, 117, 118

Barrie Morse: 15, 33, 41, 73, 81, 93

Ian Staples: 66, 70, 72

Jez Barrington: 11, 71, 104, 105

The Oxford History Centre: 34, 45, 48, 65, 69

Carol & Norman Wiles: 59, 83, 87, 97, 103, 107

Clive Sanderson: 90, 91

Banbury Guardian: 1, 31, 47, 80

The Canal & Rivers Trust: 7, 13, 16, 18, 22, 24, 25, 26, 38, 49, 106

Waterway's World: 44

David Martin, Waterway's World: 123, 124, 125, 126, 127

Kate Saffin Alarum Theatre: 112

Valerie Petts: 10

British Library: 19, 23, 89

Granny Buttons: 36

Matthew Armitage: 2, 4, 5, 8, 9, 12, 14, 17, 50, 51, 54, 56, 57, 58, 60, 61, 62, 63, 64, 74, 75, 77, 78, 82, 84, 85, 88, 92, 94, 95, 99, 100, 101, 102, 108, 109, 110, 111, 113, 115, 119, 120, 122, 128, 129, 130, 131

All other images are from Tooley's collection, many of which have been bestowed to Tooley's Boatyard. Every reasonable effort has been made to establish the copyright for all other images and sources, cover, figures 6, 20, 29, 30, 35, 37, 39, 40, 42, 52, 55, 79, 86, 96, 116